"How Sweet it is"

From the ♥ of Arkansas

PICKLES GAP VILLAGE

Southern Gateway to the Ozarks

On Scenic Highway 65 North
5-A Gap View Rd., Conway, AR 72032
(501)329-9049

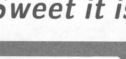

Sweet Treats, Pickles, Dips, Dressings
Sauces, & Etc., From Janis Mack
Pickles Gap Village, Conway, AR

Cook Book

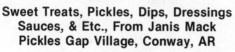

To order additional books write or call:

5-A Gapview Road
Highway 65 North
Conway, AR 72032

Attention: Janis Mack

(501) 329-9049   FAX (501) 327-0511
(See order form in back)

Printed in the USA by:
Enterprise Printing Company, Inc.
Jim and Kathy Johnson
P.O. Box 258 - Highway 178
Bull Shoals, Arkansas 72619

Janis Mack

The Lord is my rock, and my fortress, and my deliverer; my God, my strength, in whom I will trust; my buckler, and the horn of my salvation, and my high tower.

Psalms 18: 2

Acknowledgement & Expression of Appreciation . . . .

Thanks to friends and family members who have contributed their treasured recipes for this cook book.

Special Thanks . . . .

To my secretary, Bonnie Steenis, for all the help she gave me in compiling and typing these recipes. Bonnie has been a loyal employee for several years and we appreciate her very much.

To the artist, Rita Hood, a very gifted lady that did the cute illustrations throughout the cook book.

Janis Mack

Dedication . . . .

I dedicate this book to by husband, Ralph L. Mack, Jr. and to my mother, Esther Howard, who is one of the best southern cooks in Arkansas. (You will find a lot of her recipes in this cook book.) And also to the memory of my loving father, Exel Howard. He left behind a great Christian heritage and a host of friends and fond memories. A lot of his favorite quotes can be found in this book.

Ralph Mack, right, is happiest when he is in the knife corner at Mack's General Store, Pickles Gap Village.

Exel and Esther Howard as they celebrated their 50th Wedding Anniversary.

50 YEARS TOGETHER

We have enjoyed 50 years of marriage
Sometimes the road was rough
That road was made much smoother
For there was love enough.

We have always trusted God
Thanked Him for each other
Hope we have set a good example
As a father and a mother.

He does many things for me
But seldom open doors
I don't care about those things
For he is so good at mopping floors.

A very loving husband
A special kind of dad
Wish we had 50 more years together
Just like the ones we had.

Esther Howard
Greenbrier

Appetizers & Beverages

Arkansas Post Family Muscadine Juice and Jellies are available at the Pickle Barrel Restaurant & Sweet Shop at Pickles Gap Village. Write for a mail order form or call 501-327-7708. We ship!

Santa always comes to Pickles Gap, thanks to Santa's helper John Tyrrell.

A lovely family enjoying a treat at the Pickle Barrel at Pickles Gap Village.

Arkansas Style Frog Legs

1 pound frog legs
(4 to 6 pairs per pound)

Salted water

2 cups buttermilk

2 cups seasoned flour

Soak frog legs in salted water for 2 hours; drain. Dip frog legs in buttermilk and roll in seasoned flour. Deep-fry for 7 to 8 minutes. Do not crowd. Fry 2 to 3 pairs at a time. Drain and serve immediately. Serves 2.

(This Little Frog Critter in photo is featured on one of the PICKLES GAP T-SHIRTS offered for sale at Pickles Gap Village. Write for our mail order brochure.)

Low-Fat Party Mix

Note: You will need a small clean spray bottle.

3 cups Rice Chex

3 cups Corn Chex

3 cups Cheerios

3 cups fat-free pretzels

Worcestershire sauce

Buttermist

Seasoned salt

Garlic powder

Onion powder, (optional)

Preheat oven to 200 degrees. In large pan, combine cereals and pretzels. Pour Worcestershire in small spray bottle. Lightly spray top of cereal mixture with Worcestershire, then Buttermist. Lightly sprinkle seasoned salt, garlic and onion powder. Stir; repeat process several times. (Don't use too much seasoned salt.) Bake for 1-1/2 hours, stirring every 30 minutes. Allow to cool; store in air-tight container. Serves 6.

1

Low-Fat Walnut-Raisin Cream Cheese

12-ounces Kraft fat-free cream cheese

1/3 cup brown sugar

1/8 cup black walnut pieces, chopped fine

1/3 cup raisins

In medium bowl, combine ingredients; mix with electric mixer until sugar is dissolved. Refrigerate a few hours before serving. Makes 6 servings-2 tablespoons each. Try this on a cinnamon-raisin bagel!

Low-Fat Oriental Meatballs

Meatballs:

1 pound ground chicken breast or turkey breast

8-ounce can crushed pineapple, drained

3/4 cup cooked rice

1 egg white, slightly beaten

1 carrot, grated

1/3 cup chopped bell pepper

1 tablespoon Lite soy sauce

2 teaspoons dry onion flakes

Sweet and Sour Sauce:

18-ounce jar orange marmalade

2 teaspoons Lite soy sauce

1 tablespoon vinegar

Preheat oven to 375 degrees.

Combine meatball ingredients; form into 1" balls. Bake on baking sheet sprayed with nonstick cooking spray for 20 minutes or until brown. In small bowl, combine all sauce ingredients. Use as dip for meatballs or spoon over top when served. Serves 8.

Low-Fat Mexican Layered Dip

1 pound ground turkey breast or chicken breast

1 package dry taco seasoning

1/2 cup water

16-ounce can fat-free refried beans

4-ounce can chopped green chilies

1 small onion, chopped

1 cup fat-free sour cream

1/2 cup fat-free cheese, grated

1 large tomato, chopped opt.

Brown ground turkey in skillet sprayed with nonstick cooking spray. Add taco seasoning and water; simmer and stir until all water is cooked away. Set aside to cool. Spread refried beans evenly over bottom of 8" or 9" round or square baking dish. Layer with meat, chilies, onion and sour cream. Top with grated cheese and tomatoes. Chill; serve with no-oil tortilla chips. Makes 8 servings.

Low Calorie Mock French Onion Dip

1 large cottage cheese

2 packages Weight Watchers onion broth

1/4 cup minced onions

2 tablespoons celery and parsley flakes

1/2 teaspoon paprika

Black pepper to taste

1/4 cup water

1 tablespoon lemon juice

Place all ingredients into a blender or food processor; blend until smooth and creamy. Chill in refrigerator at least an hour before serving.

Margarett Bono

Low-Fat Green Chile Queso

4 slices Kraft fat-free cheddar cheese

1 can green chile enchilada sauce

1/2 cup stewed tomatoes, chopped

4-ounce can green chilies, chopped

2 teaspoons dry onion flakes

1 clove garlic, pressed or 1/4 teaspoon garlic powder

In food processor, blend cheese and enchilada sauce until smooth. Combine with remaining ingredients and simmer in saucepan until heated. Serve warm with no-oil tortilla chips. Makes 8 servings. NOTE: Warm over very low heat. If heat is too high, cheese begins to separate and curdle.

Bar-B-Cups

3/4 pound ground beef

1/2 cup barbecue sauce

2 tablespoons brown sugar

1 tablespoon minced onion

1 can Pillsbury refrigerated, tenderflake biscuits

3/4 cup shredded Cheddar cheese

Brown beef and drain. Add barbecue sauce, brown sugar and onion. Separate each biscuit and cut in half. Place each biscuit in an ungreased, tiny muffin tin cup, pressing dough up sides and on bottom. Fill with meat mixture. Bake at 400 degrees for 8 minutes or until golden brown. Sprinkle with cheese while still hot.

Marj Hohnbaum

Blender Potato Pancakes

3 cups raw potatoes, cubed
2 eggs
1/4 cup flour
1 small onion, quartered
1 teaspoon salt
1/4 teaspoon baking powder

Wash, peel and cut up potatoes. Pat dry with paper towel. Put all ingredients into blender. Cover. Press "chop" button for 10 seconds. Use spatula to push potatoes down if necessary. (Stop motor when using spatula.) Pour batter onto hot greased griddle, about 1/4 cup for each pancake. Brown and turn once to brown other side. Makes 4 servings.

Nacho Popcorn

5 tablespoons margarine
1 teaspoon paprika
1/2 teaspoon crushed red pepper
1/2 teaspoon ground cumin
11 cups popped popcorn
6 tablespoons grated Parmesan cheese

In a saucepan, melt margarine. Stir the paprika, red pepper and cumin into the margarine. Let cool for about 5 minutes. Place popcorn in large bowl; pour spice mixture on top; sprinkle with cheese. Toss until popcorn is coated.

Spanish Potato Omelet

6 small potatoes
3 medium onions
6 to 8-ounces smoked ham
12 eggs
Salt and pepper to taste
Oil

Slice potatoes, onions and ham with thinnest slicing disc on food processor or slice as thinly as possible by hand. Sauté potatoes and onions in oil until soft, but not brown. Butter an 11-3/4x7-1/2 inch glass baking dish. Layer ingredients in dish. Scramble eggs; pour over all. Bake at 325 degree oven for 20-25 minutes, or until eggs are set. Cut into squares. Makes 6 servings.

Party Mix

1 box each of Corn Chex, Rice Chex, Cheerios
1 box pretzels
1 can shoestring potatoes
Nuts
2 cups salad oil
1 tablespoon brown sugar
2 tablespoons Worcestershire
1 tablespoon garlic salt

Combine dry ingredients. Add liquid and bake in oven at 250 degrees for 1-1/2 hours, stirring frequently.

Cheese Sticks

1 cup flour
1-1/2 teaspoons baking powder
1/2 teaspoon salt
2 tablespoons butter or margarine
1/2 cup shredded sharp Cheddar
1/3 cup cold water

Sift flour, baking powder and salt into medium bowl. Cut in butter or margarine with pastry cutter until mixture is crumbly. Add cheese. Toss until well blended. Sprinkle water over mixture; mix lightly with fork until pastry holds together and leaves the side of the bowl clean. Roll on a floured surface into a 12x10-inch rectangle. Cut in half lengthwise; then cut each half crosswise into 1/2-inch strips. Lift strips one at at time, twist and place 1-inch apart on an ungreased cookie sheet. Bake at 425 degrees for 10 minutes or until lightly golden. Cool before serving. Makes 4 dozen.

Markie's Cheese Ball

1 pound grated Velveeta cheese
8 strips bacon, crumbled
(fry crisp and cool)
7 green onions, chopped
2 ounces slivered almonds, toasted
4 tablespoons Hellman's mayonnaise

Mix together and shape into a ball. Can be rolled in chili powder or paprika for added color.

Jan Barrow

Cucumbers Stuffed with Ham

2 cucumbers
French dressing
2 cups cooked ham, diced
2 tablespoons cream cheese
4 tablespoons light cream
Horseradish to taste
Pepper to taste
Shrimp (optional)

Peel cucumbers, cut in half lengthwise; scoop out seeds, leaving boat-shaped cases. Marinate cucumbers in dressing for at least 1 hour. Combine cream cheese, cream, horseradish, and pepper; add ham; fill cucumbers with mixture. Garnish with shrimp. Serves 4.

Dill Dip

1 cup mayonnaise
2 tablespoons grated onion
2 tablespoons Beau Monde
1 cup sour cream
2 tablespoons dried parsley
1 tablespoons dill

Mix all ingredients and chill. This dip is great on vegetables and chips!

5

Fiesta Bean Dip

2 cups hot cooked pinto beans mashed
1 large clove garlic, mashed
1 tablespoon jalapeno liquid
2 cups sharp Cheddar, grated
2 tablespoons minced onion
1 jalapeno pepper, diced fine

Combine beans and enough bean liquid to make a dipping consistency in saucepan. Add remaining ingredients, mixing well. Cook over low heat until cheese is melted. Serve hot with tortillas or chips.

Chili-Cheese Dip

1 pound lean ground beef
8-ounce can Rotel Green Chilies
1/2 to 1 teaspoon chili pepper
1 pound grated, processed American cheese
2 teaspoons Worcestershire

Brown ground beef well and drain off excess grease. Put ground beef and all remaining ingredients in crock pot or slow cooker. Stir well. Cover and cook on high for one hour, stirring until the cheese is fully melted. Serve immediately or turn to low for serving up to six hours. Serve with tortilla or corn chips. For thicker dip, stir in paste of: 2 tablespoons flour and 3 tablespoons water. For thinner dip, add milk.

Mexican Cheese Dip

5 tablespoons margarine, melted
5-1/3 tablespoons flour

Cook above in double boiler for 1 minute, then add:

1-1/3 teaspoons paprika
2 teaspoons chili powder
1-1/3 teaspoons ketchup
1-1/3 tablespoons juice of jalapeno pepper
1/3 teaspoon dry mustard
1-1/3 teaspoons cumin
2/3 jalapeno pepper, diced fine
8-ounces American cheese, cubed

Mix the listed ingredients and add to margarine and flour. Cook until cheese melts. Add 2-1/3 cups milk and 3 shakes of garlic powder. Cook over low heat, stirring constantly.

Deep Fried Squash

Squash
Buttermilk
Self-rising flour
Hot oil
Salt

Slice squash thin; salt and let set for 30 minutes. Drain off liquid. Wet with buttermilk, drain. Dip in self-rising flour; drop into hot oil until brown. Serve hot.   **Esther Howard**

Green Fried Tomatoes

1 clove garlic, minced
1 tablespoon parsley, chopped
1/2 teaspoon salt
Dash pepper
1 onion, minced
1 tablespoon vegetable oil
2 large green tomatoes, thickly sliced
1 cup cornmeal

Combine garlic, parsley, salt, pepper, onion, and oil. Spread mixture on tomato slices, sprinkle with cornmeal; sauté in lightly oiled skillet until heated through and browned. Makes 4 servings.

Mexican Bean Dip

15-1/2 ounce can mashed refried beans
10-ounce can Rotel tomatoes and chilies
1/4 pound Velveeta cheese, grated
1 teaspoon cumin
1/4 teaspoon chili powder

Heat beans, tomatoes, and cheese in a double boiler. Add cumin and cook slowly about 30 minutes or until smooth. Add chili powder only if you desire a more fiery dip. Serve in a chafing dish with tortillas or corn chips. Serves 8.

Batter Dip for Vegetables

1/4 cup flour
1/2 cup cornstarch
1 teaspoon baking powder
1/2 teaspoon salt
1/4 teaspoon pepper
1/2 cup water (beer is better)
1 egg, beaten

In a bowl, stir first six ingredients. Add beaten egg until batter is smooth. Dip vegetables and deep fry until golden brown. For herb batter, add 1 teaspoon dried basil, cloves of garlic, and minced onion.

Chipped Beef Dip

2 packages cream cheese
1 cup sour cream
2 tablespoons milk
1 tablespoon Worcestershire
3/4 cup green onion, diced fine
3/4 cup green pepper, diced fine
6-ounce package dried beef, diced
Garlic salt to taste

Mix cheese, cream and milk all together. Add remaining ingredients. Stir well. Serve with chips.

"A heart filled with love always overflows."

7

Spinach Dip

1 package frozen spinach, chopped

1 can water chestnuts

3 tablespoons mayonnaise

2 cups sour cream

3 green onions, chopped

1/2 teaspoon salt

1 package dry vegetable soup mix

Drain water chestnuts and thaw spinach. Chop and mix all ingredients together. Refrigerate for about one hour before serving.

Fruit Dip

16-ounces marshmallow creme

8-ounce package cream cheese

Combine ingredients and mix thoroughly. Serve with your favorite sliced fruits.

Corn Dogs

1 cup corn meal

1 cup flour

2 tablespoons sugar

2 teaspoons baking powder

1/2 teaspoon salt

1 egg, slightly beaten

1 cup milk

2 tablespoons melted shortening

1 pound weiners

Mix corn meal with flour, sugar, baking powder and salt. Add egg and milk; blend in melted shortening. Mix well. Dip wieners in batter. Fry in deep fat.

Vegetable Pizza

2 large cans crescent rolls

2 (8-ounce) packages cream cheese

1 cup mayonnaise or Miracle Whip

1 package Hidden Valley Party Dip Mix

3/4 cup grated Cheddar

3/4 cup each finely chopped cauliflower, broccoli, carrots, green pepper, green onion

Preheat oven to 375 degrees. Place crescent roll dough in bottom of a large ungreased jelly roll pan. Press to seal edges together. Bake 8-10 minutes until golden brown. Set aside to cool. Combine softened cream cheese, mayonnaise, and dip mix. Blend well and spread over cooled crust. Top with grated cheese. Combine all the vegetables and sprinkle over cheese. Cut into squares to serve.

Cloedean Scroggins

8

Helpful Hints   for Coffee Making

• Allow 3/4 cup water per serving to 2 tablespoons coffee for most types of coffee makers. (For stronger coffee use 3 tablespoons coffee per 3/4 cup water.) Strength may be varied by increasing or decreasing one or the other ingredient.

• Freshly ground coffee is best. Never combine old coffee with newly purchased coffee.

• Begin with cold water when preparing coffee.

• Never allow coffee to boil.

• Serve coffee immediately (the flavor deteriorates when coffee is kept warm for longer than one hour) and do not reheat.

• Remove coffee grounds as soon as coffee is brewed.

• Always clean coffee residue from utensils to prevent bitter tasting coffee. A bitter taste often results from the chemical action of the coffee creating a substance which clings to the interior of the pot.

• Cafeau Lait — Brew strong black coffee. Simultaneously pour coffee and an equal amount of scalded milk into cup. Add sugar if desired.

• Cappuccino — Italian steamed coffee. Add 1/2 cup scalded milk to 1 cup hot espresso. In a warm bowl, beat milk and espresso until foamy. Sugar may be added if desired. Pour into cup and sprinkle with cinnamon.

• Demitasse — Brew double strength coffee. Serve in small cups. Sprinkle bits of chocolate in cup for a mocha flavor.

• Dessert coffees are very rich. Serve them in tall tempered glasses.

Summertime Tea Punch

4-6 tea bags
6-ounce can frozen orange juice
6-ounce can frozen lemonade
1-1/2 cups sugar

Make tea as usual. Dump all the above in a one gallon container. Add enough water to make one gallon.

Becky Poe

Swisse Mocha

1/2 cup instant coffee
1 cup nonfat dry milk powder
1/2 cup sugar
2 tablespoons unsweetened cocoa

Combine all ingredients. Place four rounded teaspoons in one cup and add 3/4 to 1 cup boiling water. Calories: 40 per cup.

"Kindness is Christianity with its work clothes on."

9

Exotic Coffee
Cafe Vienna

1/2 cup instant coffee

2/3 cup nonfat dry milk powder

2/3 cup sugar

1/2 teaspoon cinnamon

Combine all ingredients. Place four rounded teaspoons in cup and add 3/4 to 1 cup boiling water. Makes about 2 cups of dry mix, or enough to make 20 cups of coffee. Calories: 35 per cup.

Cafe Cappucciano

1/2 cup instant coffee

1 cup nonfat dry milk powder

3/4 cup sugar

1/2 teaspoon dried orange peel, crushed in a bowl with a spoon

Combine all ingredients. Place four rounded teaspoons in cup and add 3/4 to 1 cup boiling water. Calories: 40 per cup.

Hot Spiced Cider

2 quarts apple juice

1/2 cup brown sugar

1/4 teaspoon salt

1 whole stick cinnamon

1 teaspoon whole allspice

1 teaspoon whole cloves

Combine cider, brown sugar, and salt in saucepan. Add spices. Slowly bring to simmering. Cover and simmer 20 minutes. Remove spices with slotted spoon. Serve hot. Spices can be put in a loose tea shell.

Cranberry Appleteaser

8 cups (2 quarts) cranberry juice cocktail

8 cups orange juice

2 lemons, thinly sliced

4 tablespoons sugar

1 teaspoon cinnamon

1/2 teaspoon nutmeg

To serve hot: mix all ingredients and simmer slowly for 10 minutes. Remove lemon slices; garnish with orange slices. To serve cold: simmer lemon, sugar, spices with 2 cups of the cranberry juice. Add remaining fruit juices...chill and serve over ice mold or cubes.

Spiced Coffee Punch

1 quart milk

1 quart strong brewed coffee

1/2 cup sugar

Dash of ground cinnamon

3 whole cloves

1 pint vanilla ice cream

Several drops almond extract

Scald milk. Add coffee, sugar and spices. Chill. Put ice cream which has been scooped into small pieces into punch bowl. Add coffee and milk mixture and almond extract. Stir to mix. Serves 12.

Delicious Coffee Punch

4 *quarts strong coffee*

5 *teaspoons vanilla*

5 *tablespoons sugar*

1 *quart whipping cream, whipped and chilled*

2 *quarts (or more) vanilla ice cream*

Prepare coffee. Add vanilla and sugar. Chill. Before serving spoon ice cream into punch bowl. Add coffee mixture and fold in whipped cream. Mix well. Taste before serving and add more sugar if needed. Serves 50.

Hollins Coffee

1/2 *gallon cold strong coffee*

2 *teaspoons vanilla*

1 *teaspoon cinnamon*

1/2 *gallon chocolate ice cream*

1/2 *gallon vanilla ice cream*

1 *pint heavy cream, whipped*

Combine coffee, vanilla, and cinnamon; chill well. When ready to serve, pour coffee into a large punch bowl. Spoon in ice cream in chunks. Fold in whipped cream and serve immediately. Makes approximately 1-1/4 gallons.

"God gives his very best to those who leave the choice with him."

Fireside Coffee

2 *cups cocoa mix*

2 *cups instant non-dairy creamer*

1 *cup instant coffee granules*

1-1/2 *cups powdered sugar*

3/4 *teaspoon cinnamon*

3/4 *teaspoon nutmeg*

Using a large container with a lid, mix all ingredients well. To serve, place three to four teaspoons of the mixture in a mug and fill with hot water. Makes 6-1/2 cups of mix.

Irish Coffee Mix

1 *package butter mints*

2 *cups chocolate malted milk mix*

1/2 *cup Nestlé's Quick*

6-*ounces non-dairy creamer*

4-*ounces instant coffee granules*

In a food processor or blender, blend mints and malted milk mix until very fine. Mix this and other ingreadients in a storage container with a tight cover. Store. To serve, add three to four tablespoons of mix to 1 cup hot water, stirring well. For an extra zing, add Irish whiskey, amaretto, cognac, etc. Also may be topped with ice cream or whipped cream. Makes 4-5 cups of mix.

Punch the way you like it. . .Ladies do your thing! You can keep adding until it tastes just right!!

Party Punch

2 cans Hawaiian Punch

1 quart ginger ale

1 cup pineapple juice

1/2 gallon vanilla ice cream

Chill all ingredients. Mix just before ready to use.

Fruit Punch

1 large bottle concentrated Hawaiian Punch

2 large bottles of 7-up

Raspberry sherbet, or your flavor of choice

Mix the concentrated Hawaiian Punch with water to taste. Add about 2 large bottles of 7-Up, or to taste. Spoon tablespoons of sherbet or cut sherbet into chunks and add to bowl. Delicious!

Red Punch

1 large can pineapple juice

1-1/2 cups sugar

2 packages cherry Kool-Aid unsweetened

Mix all ingredients together. Add enough water to make a gallon. Ginger ale may be added in addition to the water. Serve over ice or freeze until slushy.

Punch

2 quarts orange Kool-Aid

1 quart ginger ale

1/2 gallon pineapple sherbet

Mix and serve. You can freeze 2 quarts of orange Kool-Aid in a mold ahead of time to suit whatever the occasion may be. Then when ready to serve, put this in punch. That way it keeps it cold and doesn't weaken the taste of the punch.

Punch

1 package orange Kool-Aid

2 cups sugar

1 package raspberry Kool-Aid

1 pint pineapple juice

Add water to make 1 gallon or add part ginger ale. Freeze cubes of Kool-Aid .... it adds color and flavor. This recipe tastes like Hawaiian Punch and is inexpensive.

12

Sparkling Punch

6-ounce can frozen lemonade concentrate, thawed and undiluted

3 quarts ginger ale, chilled

8-ounce can crushed pineapple, undrained

10-ounce package frozen strawberries, thawed and undrained

Combine all ingredients except ginger ale in container of electric blender. Blend at high speed for 30 seconds, or until smooth. Just before serving, stir in ginger ale. Makes about 4 quarts.

Banana Punch

8 cups water

2 (46-ounce) cans pineapple juice

1/2 cup lemon juice (fresh or bottled)

4 cups sugar

4 (6-ounce) cans frozen orange juice

5 large bananas, mashed

2 quarts ginger ale

Boil sugar and water for 15 minutes; let cool. Dilute orange juice as directed. Mix sugar and water solution, bananas, orange juice and pineapple juice and freeze. Thaw 4 to 6 hours or to a slush. Pour ginger ale over mixture in punch bowl. Makes 50 to 60 servings. Frozen mix keeps for weeks.

Lemon-Strawberry Punch

3 (6-ounce) cans frozen lemonade concentrate

1 quart ginger ale, chilled

10-ounce package frozen strawberries, thawed

In a large punch bowl, prepare lemonade concentrate as directed on can; stir in strawberries (in syrup). Stir in ginger ale and, if you wish, add small scoops of strawberry ice cream. Makes 28 (1/2 cup) servings.

Mardi Gras Punch

6-ounce can frozen orange juice concentrate, thawed

1 quart apple juice, chilled

Raspberry, orange, lime and lemon sherbet

6-ounce can frozen lemonade concentrate, thawed

2 quarts ginger ale, chilled

In a large punch bowl, stir together concentrates and apple juice. Stir in ginger ale; scoop sherbet into balls and spoon into punch. Makes fourteen 1 cup servings.

Wedding Punch

2-1/2 cups pineapple juice, chilled

1 pint lime, lemon or raspberry sherbet

1 pint vanilla ice cream

12-ounce bottle ginger ale or 7-Up

Combine pineapple juice, sherbet and 1/2 of ice cream. Beat until smooth. Add 7-Up or ginger ale. Spoon remaining ice cream into punch. Serve immediately. Makes 14 (1/2 cup) servings.

Party Punch (Yellow)

1 large can pineapple juice

1 large can apricot nectar

2 packages lemon kool-aid

1 large can crushed pineapple

2 cups sugar or to taste

32-ounces 7-Up, cold

Mix Kool-Aid as directed on package. Add the remaining ingredients—except 7-Up. Put in freezer, stir to make slush. Pour 7-Up over punch when ready to serve.

Instant Hot Drink

1-pound jar of instant breakfast orange drink

1/2 cup instant tea

1 cup instant lemonade drink mix

1 cup sugar

2 teaspoons cinnamon

1 teaspoon ground cloves

1 cup red hots

Mix dry ingredients and store in air-tight container. Add 3 tablespoons of mix to a cup of hot water.

Hot Percolator Punch

2 cups cranberry juice

2 cups pineapple juice

1/3 cup brown sugar

1 cup water

1 tablespoon whole cloves

2 sticks cinnamon (broken up)

1/4 teaspoon salt

Dissolve sugar in water. Pour juice and sugar mixture in percolator. Place cloves and cinnamon in basket. Perk through cycle.

We offer Post Family Muscadine Juices & Jellies for sale at Pickles Gap Village.

14

BREADS & SWEET ROLLS

(We have wonderful apple butter, jams, and jellies available at Pickles Gap Village. Write for mail order brochure or call 501-327-7708.)

The Pickle Barrel is a favorite place for birthday celebrations. "What a neat place to break bread together."

Low-Fat Pumpkin Gingerbread

1/2 cup packed, light brown sugar

2 tablespoons sugar

1/4 cup liquid Butter Buds

Grated peel of 1/2 orange

3 Egg Beaters

1 can solid-pack pumpkin

1/4 cup water

1/4 cup light corn syrup

2 tablespoons molasses

1-1/4 cups cake flour

1/2 teaspoon baking powder

1 teaspoon baking soda

1/2 teaspoon cinnamon

1/2 teaspoon ginger

1/4 teaspoon nutmeg

1/4 teaspoon ground cloves

1/4 teaspoon lite salt, optional

Vanilla Sauce:

2 cups skim milk

1 Egg Beater

3/4 cup sugar

1 teaspoon vanilla

Dash of nutmeg

1 tablespoon flour or 2 teaspoons cornstarch

1 teaspoon liquid Butter Buds

Place rack in center of oven. Preheat oven to 350 degrees. Spray an 8-inch square baking dish with non-fat cooking spray.

Use the mixer to cream sugars, liquid Butter Buds, and Egg Beaters until smooth. Beat about two minutes. Mix in pumpkin, water, corn syrup, and molasses on medium speed until smooth. Sift together flour, baking soda, baking powder, lite salt, cinnamon, ginger, nutmeg and cloves; add gradually to the batter blending well with hand mixer. Transfer batter to prepared pan. Bake 30 minutes, or until toothpick inserted in center comes out clean. Do not overbake. Let cool on rack at least 15 minutes. Serve with warm vanilla sauce.

Vanilla Sauce:

Boil milk and beat in sugar, flour, and Egg Beater that have been mixed together. Simmer until it thickens, stirring constantly. Remove from heat and stir in vanilla and liquid Butter Buds. Stir in a dash of nutmeg. Serves 9.

Low-Fat Delicious Gingerbread with Sauce

1/2 cup liquid Butter Buds

1/2 cup molasses

1 teaspoon ginger

2 teaspoons allspice

2 teaspoons cinnamon

2 teaspoons nutmeg

(continued on next page)

(continued from previous page)

2 teaspoons soda, dissolved in 1 cup boiling water

1/2 cup sugar

2-1/2 cups flour

2 Egg Beaters

Cream Butter Buds and sugar; add remaining ingredients; add Egg Beaters last. Spray either a bundt or tube pan with non-fat cooking spray. Bake 35-40 minutes at 350 degrees. Serve warm with sauce of your choice.

Vanilla Sauce:

2 cups skim milk

1 Egg Beater

3/4 cup sugar

1 teaspoon vanilla

Dash nutmeg

1 tablespoon flour or 2 teaspoons cornstarch

Boil milk. Mix sugar, flour and Egg Beater; add to milk. Simmer until it thickens, stirring constantly. Remove from heat; add vanilla and nutmeg.

Caramel Sauce:

2 Egg Beaters

1 cup skim evaporated milk

1 pound brown sugar

1 tablespoon liquid Butter Buds

1 teaspoon vanilla

1 tablespoon flour or 2 teaspoons cornstarch

Add Egg Beaters and

skim milk to sugar in top of double boiler. Cook until creamy, adding flour slowly. Add Butter Buds. Remove from heat and stir in vanilla. Serves 10-12.

Low-Fat Orange Breakfast Rolls

Rolls:

6-ounce can frozen orange juice concentrate, thawed

Grated peel from 1/2 orange

7-1/2 ounce can refrigerated biscuits (find one with 1 gram fat per biscuit)

1/2 teaspoon Molly McButter

1 tablespoon sugar

Preheat oven to 350 degrees. Save one tablespoon orange juice concentrate for icing. Mix remaining concentrate with orange zest. Dip biscuits in concentrate; place in square or round baking dish sprayed with nonstick cooking spray. Sprinkle tops with Molly McButter and sugar. Bake for 30 minutes. Remove from oven; pour icing over while hot.

Icing:

3/4 cup powdered sugar

1/4 cup fat-free cream cheese

1 tablespoon orange juice concentrate

Zest from 1/2 orange

1/2 teaspoon Molly McButter

Combine all ingredients and mix well. Makes 8 servings.

Cotton Pickin' Corn Bread

As served at the Pickle Barrel - Pickles Gap Village

1 package Cotton Pickin' corn meal mix
1/2 cup self-rising cornmeal
2 eggs
3 large tablespoons sour cream
1/2 cup cream style corn
1/4 cup salad oil
1/4 cup milk

Mix well. Let set 10 minutes after pouring into muffin tins. Bake at 350 degrees for approximately 15 to 20 minutes until done.

Esther Howard

This is a favorite served with brown beans and ham at the restaurant.

Sour Cream Cornbread

1 cup self-rising cornmeal
1 heaping tablespoon self-rising flour
1/2 cup sour cream
8-3/4 ounce can cream style corn
2 eggs
1/4 cup vegetable oil or peanut oil
1 tablespoon milk

Mix well; pour into muffin pans. Bake at approximately 350 degrees for approximately 30 minutes. Makes 16 muffins. For a different flavor, add 1 teaspoon chopped jalapeno peppers.

Esther Howard

Broccoli Cornbread

2 boxes Jiffy Cornbread Mix
8-ounces sour cream or cottage cheese
4 eggs
10-ounce package chopped frozen broccoli
1/2 stick margarine

Cook broccoli in microwave with 2 tablespoons water for 5 to 10 minutes. Mix all ingredients, except margarine. Melt margarine; pour into 9x13 inch baking dish. Pour in mixture; bake 375 degrees until done. For added flavor add 1/3 cup sauted onion and 3/4 cup grated Cheddar cheese to mixture before baking.

Esther Howard

Mexican Cornbread

1 cup white cornmeal
1/2 cup flour
1/2 teaspoon each soda and baking powder
1 teaspoon salt
2 tablespoons chopped onions
1 jalapeno pepper & 1 pimento pepper, chopped
1/2 cup whole kernel corn
1 egg
1 cup buttermilk

Mix all ingredients. Pour in well greased pan; bake in hot oven.

Zucchini Bread
(Two Loaves)

3 eggs

2 cups sugar

1 cup oil

2 teaspoons vanilla

2 cups zucchini squash, peeled and grated

3 cups flour

1 teaspoon salt

1 teaspoon baking powder

1/2 teaspoon cinnamon

1 cup nuts, optional

Beat eggs, sugar, oil and vanilla. Add zucchini, then flour sifted with salt, baking powder and cinnamon. Add 1 cup nuts, more or less. Bake at 350 degrees in two greased and floured loaf pans for 1 hour. (Glass pans-325 degrees.)

Mexican Cornbread

1 cup yellow cornmeal

1/2 teaspoon salt

1/2 teaspoon soda

1/3 cup melted shortening

1 cup sour cream

8-ounce can cream-style corn

2 eggs, beaten

1 cup shredded Cheddar cheese

4-ounce can chopped green chiles, drained

Combine cornmeal, salt and soda; blend. Stir in shortening; add sour cream, corn, and eggs. Mix well. Add green chiles, cheese and stir. Pour in greased 9x13-inch pan and bake at 375 degrees for 35 to 40 minutes.

Corn Fritters

1 cup flour

1/4 cup milk

1 teaspoon baking powder

2 eggs

3/4 teaspoon salt

2 tablespoons Crisco

1-1/2 cups whole kernel corn, drained

Sift dry ingredients together. Beat eggs well; add milk and combine with first mixture. Beat thoroughly. Add corn and melted Crisco. Drop by teaspoon into deep hot oil. Cook until golden brown.

Mary Gill

Mary Gill was a very dear friend and employee of mine. She has gone to be with the Lord, but left behind a lot of friends and sweet memories. We miss her!

Janis Mack

18

Corn Fritters

Another version by my friend, Charlotte Roberts

1-1/4 cups Bisquick
1 tablespoon salt
2 eggs
2 tablespoons cornmeal
Cream Style Corn

Mix first four ingredients together. Add enough corn to make a stiff batter. Drop by teaspoon into hot oil. Cook until golden brown. Delicious served with honey.

Onion-Cheese Supper Bread

1/2 cup onion, chopped
1 tablespoon shortening
1 egg, slightly beaten
1/2 cup milk
1-1/2 cups Bisquick
1 cup sharp cheese, grated
1 tablespoon poppy seeds
2 tablespoons butter, melted

Heat oven to 400 degrees. Sauté onion in shortening until golden. Mix egg and milk; blend in Bisquick. Add onion and half of the cheese. Spread dough in greased 8x1-1/2 inch round glass baking dish. Sprinkle top with remaining cheese and poppy seed. Sprinkle melted butter over all. Bake 20 to 25 minutes. Serve hot. Makes 6 to 8 servings.

Magic Biscuits

5 cups plain flour
1 teaspoon soda
3 teaspoons baking powder
1 teaspoon salt
4 tablespoons sugar
1 cup shortening
2 cups buttermilk
1 package dry yeast
4 tablespoons hot water

Mix dry ingredients; cut in shortening. Add buttermilk and yeast that has been dissolved in hot water. Put in oiled bowl in refrigerator. You don't have to wait for rising. Roll out and cut with biscuit cutter. Bake at 425 degrees for 10 minutes.
Note:
1) Better second day.
2) Use only amount needed.
3) Will keep a week in refrigerator.

Angel Biscuits

5 cups white flour unsifted

1 teaspoon soda

3 teaspoons baking powder

1 teaspoon salt

1/4 to 1/2 cup sugar

1 cup shortening

1 package yeast

2 cups buttermilk

Dissolve yeast in 1/4 cup lukewarm water. Sift all dry ingredients together. Cut in shortening; add yeast, water and buttermilk. Place in covered bowl in refrigerator overnight. Bake as needed. On floured board roll 1/2-inch thick and cut with a biscuit cutter. Bake at 400 degrees for 12 to 15 minutes. Makes 3 to 5 dozen.

Southern Biscuits

1 cup plus 2 tablespoons flour

1 teaspoon baking powder

1/2 teaspoon salt

1/4 teaspoon baking soda

2 tablespoons Crisco or butter

1/2 cup buttermilk

1 tablespoon Crisco for frying pan

Mix the dry ingredients together in a mixing bowl. Blend in the Crisco until the mixture is coarse and grainy, using a pastry cutter. Stir in buttermilk. Do not over mix. Put on a floured board and knead just a few times. Pat out the dough to about 1/2" thickness. Cut with a floured biscuit cutter or a glass. Do not handle the dough too much or it will get tough. Place 1 tablespoon of Crisco in a heavy black iron frying pan and put the pan in the oven at 500 degrees for about 7 minutes. Remove the pan and place the biscuits in it, turning each once in the oil. Bake for 10 minutes or until golden brown.

Garlic Bread

1-1/2 cups mayonnaise

1 cup green onions, chopped

1 cup Cheddar cheese, shredded

3 cloves garlic

Mix all together and spread on half loaf of French bread, sliced into finger sticks. Put in refrigerator for 2 hours. Bake at 350 degrees for 10 minutes.

Linda Young

Zoe's Yeast Bread

2 cups water
1 teaspoon salt
1/3 cup sugar
1/3 cup vegetable oil
1 package quick rising yeast
7-1/2 to 8 cups flour

Mix first five ingredients together. Add 5 cups of flour; stir by hand. Add remaining 2-1/2 or 3 cups flour; stir and mix by hand; add a little oil to outside of bread and sides of bowl to prevent sticking. Cover; let stand in warm place 2 to 4 hours or until doubled in size. Knead down; let stand about 1 hour. (This recipe will make 2 large loaves or a pan of cinnamon rolls. See recipe below.) For bread let rise again until doubled; you can let dough rise in warm oven. Turn oven to 350 degrees and bake until brown.

Cinnamon Rolls

Roll out bread dough whatever size pan you want and put generous amounts of softened margarine (can use Crisco), brown sugar and cinnamon. Nuts, raisins and chopped dates or whatever you prefer can be added to bread dough. Roll up bread dough and cut into 1" slices. Let rise and bake at 350 degrees until brown. Put a glaze over rolls.   *Zoe Mack*

Banana Bread

1-3/4 cups cake flour, sifted
1/4 teaspoon baking soda
1/4 cup melted shortening
Liquid sweetener to equal
1/2 cup sugar
2 teaspoons baking powder
1/4 teaspoon salt
2 eggs, well beaten
1 teaspoon vanilla
2 medium bananas, mashed

Sift together flour, baking powder, soda and salt. Combine shortening, eggs, sweetener and vanilla. Add to flour mixture; stir only until flour is moistened. Fold in mashed bananas. Place in well greased loaf pan, 8x4x3". Bake at 350 degrees for about 60 to 70 minutes. Makes 15 servings. (113 calories per serving.)

Sticky Buns

2 loaves frozen bread, thawed

2 cups brown sugar

1 large package vanilla pudding

1 stick butter, softened

1 teaspoon cinnamon

Nuts - optional

Tear one loaf thawed bread into irregular pieces; place in buttered 9x13" pan. Sprinkle mixture of brown sugar, pudding and cinnamon over the bread pieces. Tear up the second loaf of thawed bread and layer on top. Cover with wet towel and let rise about 4 hours. Bake at 350 degrees for 30 minutes. Turn upside-down immediately. Nuts and raisins may be added with the brown sugar layer.

Cracker Bread

5-1/2 to 6 cups all-purpose flour, divided

1 package dry yeast

1 teaspoon salt

2 cups warm water (105 degrees to 115 degrees)

1/3 cup butter or margarine, melted

2 tablespoons sesame seeds, toasted

Combine 4 cups flour, yeast and salt in large bowl; stir well. Gradually add water to flour mixture, stirring well. Add butter; beat at medium speed until blended. Gradually stir in enough remaining flour to make a stiff dough.

Turn dough out onto a smooth floured surface and knead until smooth and elastic - about 4 minutes. Place in a well-greased bowl, turning to grease top. Cover and let rise in a warm place (85 degrees) free from drafts, one hour or until doubled in bulk.

Punch dough down and divide into ten equal portions. Shape each portion into a ball and place on a lightly floured surface; let rest ten minutes.

Roll each ball into a 10" round on a lightly floured surface, rolling only enough to bake at one time. Chill extra dough to slow down the rising process as you await oven space. Place rolled rounds on lightly greased baking sheet. Brush lightly with cold water and sprinkle lightly with sesame seeds.

Prick entire surface with fork. Do not allow to rise. Bake at 350 degrees for 25 minutes or until lightly browned and crisp. Remove from pans, and let cool on wire racks. Repeat with remaining balls of dough. Makes 10 cracker rounds.

Becky Poe

22

Orange Butter Rolls

1 package yeast
1/4 cup warm water
1 cup sugar
1 teaspoon salt
2 eggs
1/2 cup sour cream
1/2 cup butter
2-3/4 to 3 cups flour
1 cup coconut

Soften yeast in warm water in mixing bowl. Stir in 1/4 cup sugar, salt, eggs, sour cream and 6 tablespoons butter. Gradually add flour to form a stiff dough, beating well after each addition. Cover; let rise in warm place until light and doubled, about 2 hours. Combine 3/4 cup sugar, and 3/4 cup coconut. Knead dough on well-floured surface about 15 times. Roll out half of dough to a 12" circle. Brush with 4 tablespoons melted butter. Sprinkle with half of sugar-coconut mixture. Cut into 12 wedges. Roll up starting with wide end and rolling to point. Repeat with remaining dough. Place rolls in three rows in a well-greased 13x9-inch pan. Cover, let rise in warm place until light and doubled, about 1-2 hours. Bake at 350 degrees for 25 to 30 minutes. Leave in pan. Pour glaze over hot rolls. Sprinkle with 1/4 cup coconut.

Orange Glaze

3/4 cup sugar
1/4 cup butter
1/2 cup sour cream
2 tablespoons frozen orange juice concentrate

Combine above ingredients in saucepan. Boil 3 minutes, stirring occasionally.

Charlotte Roberts

Monkey Bread

2 packages dry yeast
1 cup lukewarm water
1 cup Crisco
1 teaspoon salt
3/4 cup sugar
1 cup water
6 cups flour
2 eggs

Dissolve yeast in lukewarm water. Set aside. Heat together 1 cup Crisco, sugar, salt and 1 cup water. Let cool. Measure flour, add eggs to cooled yeast mixture. Let rise until doubled. Knead about 100 times. Roll to 1/4-inch thick; cut into all sizes then dip into melted margarine (2 sticks). Arrange in two bundt pans. Let rise until doubled; bake at 350 degrees for 30 to 35 minutes.

"If you sow kindness, you'll reap a crop of friends."

Strawberry Bread

3 cups flour
2 cups sugar
1 teaspoon salt
1 teaspoon soda
1 teaspoon cinnamon
2 cups strawberries
4 eggs, well beaten
1-1/2 cups oil
1-1/2 cups chopped nuts

Mix flour and sugar. Add salt, soda and cinnamon, then strawberries, eggs, oil and nuts. Mix well; pour into greased and floured loaf pans. Bake at 325 degrees until done. Cool; wrap; and store.

Prune Loaf

1 cup salad oil
2 cups sugar
3 eggs
2 cups flour
Dash of salt
1 teaspoon vanilla
1 cup nuts, chopped
1 cup prunes, chopped
1 teaspoon soda
1 cup buttermilk

Mix in order all but last two ingredients. Mix soda in buttermilk; add to mixture. Bake in extra large greased loaf pan 1 hour at 350 degrees

Pumpkin Bread

3-1/2 cups sifted flour
2 teaspoons soda
1-1/2 teaspoons salt
2 teaspoons cinnamon
2 teaspoons nutmeg
3 cups sugar
4 eggs, beaten
2/3 cup water
1 cup salad oil
16-ounce can pumpkin (2 cups)
1 cup pecans, chopped

Combine flour, soda, salt, cinnamon, nutmeg and sugar in large mixing bowl. Add eggs, water, oil and pumpkin; stir until blended. Add nuts; mix well. Pour mixture into three greased and floured one-pound coffee cans. Bake 1 hour at 350 degrees. Cool slightly in cans; turn out on rack to finish cooling. Flavor is best if baked day before using! This will keep for weeks in the refrigerator or freezes well. Try serving spiced tea with it!

Whether therefore ye eat, or drink, or whatsoever ye do, do all to the glory of God.

1 CORINTHIANS 10:31

There is always food, fun and fellowship at the Pickle
Barrel, Pickles Gap Village.

Italian Cream Cake

1 cup buttermilk
1 teaspoon baking soda
5 eggs, separated
2 cups sugar
1 teaspoon vanilla
3-1/2 ounce can coconut
1 cup pecans, chopped
1 stick butter
1/2 cup shortening
2 cups flour plus 1/4 teaspoon salt sifted together

Combine soda and milk. Cream sugar, butter and shortening. Add egg yolks one at a time. Beat well. Add milk and flour alternately. Stir in vanilla. Beat egg whites until stiff; fold into mixture. Stir in nuts and coconut. Bake in three 9" round cake pans for 30 minutes at 350 degrees.

Icing:
8-ounce package cream cheese
1 teaspoon vanilla
1 stick butter
1 box powdered sugar, sifted
1/3 cup pecans, chopped

Cream the cheese with butter and add the powdered sugar a little at a time. Add pecans.

Janis Mack &
Maxine Brinsfield

Devils Food Cake

2-1/2 cups flour
3 heaping tablespoons cocoa
1/2 cup butter
2 cups sugar
3 eggs
1 cup buttermilk
1/2 cup warm water
1-1/2 teaspoons soda
1-1/2 teaspoons vanilla

Sift flour with cocoa. Cream butter and add sugar, beating until creamy. Add eggs one at a time, beating well after each addition. Add buttermilk, alternating with flour mixture. Leave a little flour mixture to add to the 1/2 cup of warm water which has the soda dissolved in it. Add to mixture and add vanilla; mix well. Bake in two 9" greased cake pans at 350 degrees for 30 minutes.

Esther Howard

Coconut Cake

1 package Duncan Hines butter cake mix

Mix according to directions. Bake in three layers. Let cool.
Icing: Mix 8-ounces sour cream, 2 cups sugar, and 12 ounces frozen coconut thawed. Mix well; spread on cakes; cover with Saran Wrap. Let stand a day or so in refrigerator before cutting.

Becky Poe

Spicy Apple Sauce Cake

16-ounce can applesauce

1 cup molasses

2 teaspoons soda

4 large eggs

1-1/3 cups sugar

2/3 cup vegetable oil

3 cups flour

1/2 teaspoon salt

1 teaspoon ginger

1 teaspoon cinnamon

1/2 teaspoon cloves

Bring applesauce to boil. Stir in molasses and soda. Remove and cool. Beat eggs; add sugar; stir in oil. Combine flour and next four ingredients and add alternating to egg mixture with applesauce. Bake in 10-inch tube pan at 325 degrees for 1 hour and 15 minutes. (I double the spices in this cake. . . it tastes a lot like gingerbread!)

Rita Walker

Umm Umm Good Cake

1 yellow cake mix

15-1/4 ounce can crushed pineapple

1 cup sugar

1 small package vanilla instant pudding mix

1 cup coconut

1 small carton Cool Whip

1 cup nuts

Bake yellow cake mix as directed. While cake is cooking, mix and simmer the pineapple and sugar. While the cake is hot, punch holes in it and pour on the pineapple and sugar mixture. Mix vanilla instant pudding as directed and add the coconut. Pour over cake. Top with Cool Whip and nuts. Keep refrigerated. Very moist, better the day after.

Betty Morgan

Banana Split Cake

1 stick oleo, melted

2 cups graham cracker crumbs

Mix together and press in the bottom of a 9x13x2-inch pan; then beat:

2 eggs

2 cups powdered sugar

2 sticks oleo

Beat for 15 minutes - no less or it will water. Spread this mixture on top of crumbs. Slice 3 or 4 bananas over top of the butter mixture. Spread 1 large can of crushed pineapple, well drained, over bananas. Spread one large bowl of Cool Whip over the pineapple. Sprinkle 1 cup nuts over Cool Whip and sprinkle 1/2 cup chopped maraschino cherries over nuts. Drizzle 1/2 cup Hershey Chocolate Syrup over cherries lightly. Chill for several hours. Serves 15 to 18.

Arkansas Mockingbird Chocolate Cake

2 cups flour
2 cups sugar
1/2 teaspoon salt
2 sticks oleo
1 cup water
3 tablespoons cocoa
2 eggs, well beaten
1 teaspoon soda
1 teaspoon cinnamon
1/2 cup buttermilk
1 teaspoon vanilla

Sift flour; measure with sugar and salt. In a saucepan, put oleo, water and cocoa. Bring to a boil and pour over flour mixture. Add all other ingredients and mix well. Bake in a greased and floured shallow cake pan (15-1/2x10x1"). Bake for 20 minutes at 350 degrees. Prepare icing last five minutes cake is baking.

Icing:
Mix 1 stick oleo, 3 tablespoons cocoa, and 6 tablespoons milk in saucepan. Heat but do not boil. Remove from heat and add 1 box powdered sugar, 1/2 cup chopped pecans and 1 teaspoon vanilla. Mix and frost hot cake. *Have the coffee ready for you will want to sample while hot!*

Janis Mack

Peter Paul Mounds Cake

1 package Duncan Hines Swiss Chocolate Cake mix

Bake according to package directions in two pans. Split layers. Make filling.

Filling:
1 cup sugar
1 cup evaporated milk
1 stick margarine
14-ounce package Angel Flake coconut
24 large marshmallows

Boil sugar, milk and margarine together for 2 minutes. Remove from heat. Add marshmallows, then coconut. Divide into thirds. Cool and spread between layers. Cover cake with icing.

Icing:
1 box confectioners sugar
1/2 cup cocoa
3/4 stick margarine, softened
1/3 cup evaporated milk

Mix all ingredients together. Frost cake.

Jean Young

27

Hummingbird Cake

3 cups flour

2 cups sugar

1 teaspoon salt

1 teaspoon baking soda

1 teaspoon cinnamon

3 eggs, beaten

1-1/2 cups salad oil

1-1/2 teaspoons vanilla extract

8-ounce can crushed pineapple, undrained

2 cups chopped pecans or walnuts

2 cups chopped bannas, about 3

Combine dry ingredients in large bowl. Add eggs and oil, stirring until completely moistened. (DO NOT BEAT). Stir in vanilla, pineapple, 1 cup chopped nuts and chopped bananas. Spoon batter into three well-greased and floured 9" pans. Bake at 350 degrees for 25-30 minutes. Cool in pans 10 minutes, then remove from pans and cool completely. Frost after completely cooled.

Cream Cheese Frosting

8-ounce package cream cheese, at room temperature

1 stick margarine, room temperature

1 box powdered sugar

1 teaspoon vanilla

Combine cream cheese and butter. Cream together until smooth. Add powdered sugar and beat until light and fluffy. Stir in vanilla. Yields enough for 3 layers of cake. Sprinkle remaining 1 cup nuts over cake.

Jean Young

Strawberry Cake

4 eggs

1 white cake mix

1 package strawberry jello

1/2 cup water

3 tablespoons flour

1 cup oil

1/2 package frozen strawberries

Mix all together. Bake at 350 degrees for 25 minutes.

Icing:
Combine:

1 stick oleo

1 box powdered sugar

1/2 package frozen strawberries

Frost cake.

Gwen Allison

Texas Cake

Boil together:

2 sticks oleo

1 cup water

4 tablespoons cocoa

Cool and add:

2 cups flour

2 cups sugar

1/2 cup sour cream

1 teaspoon soda

2 eggs

1/2 teaspoon salt

Mix all together and put in a greased cookie sheet. Bake at 350 degrees for 20 minutes. Cool 15 minutes, make icing and frost.

Frosting:
Combine the following and bring just to boil:

1 stick oleo

1/4 cup milk

1 tablespoon cocoa

Add:

1 pound confectioners sugar

1 teaspoon vanilla

1 cup nuts, chopped

If too thick, add a little more milk.

Bonnie Steenis

"The man who walks with God always gets to his destination."

Orange Slice Cake

1 teaspoon soda

1 cup butter

4 eggs

3-1/2 cups flour

1 pound orange slice candy, cut fine

1/2 cup buttermilk

2 cups sugar

1 teaspoon salt

2 cups nuts, chopped

1 box dates, finely chopped

1 can shredded coconut

Dissolve soda in buttermilk. Cream butter and sugar. Add eggs one at a time. Mix well after each addition. Alternate half of the flour with the milk. Toss nuts, candy and dates with rest of flour. Add to batter and add coconut. Bake in tube pan for 2-1/2 hours at 250 degrees.

Orange Sauce:

1 cup orange juice

2 cups powdered sugar

Mix well and pour over hot cake.

Jean Young

"Failure is not defeat until you stop trying."

29

Mocha Fudge Cake

8-ounces German sweet chocolate

1 cup sugar

1 cup butter

1/2 cup strong coffee or espresso

4 eggs

1/4 cup orange marmalade or currant jelly

1 cup heavy cream

2 tablespoons instant coffee granules

1/4 cup powdered sugar

1/4 teaspoon vanilla

Combine chocolate, sugar, butter and coffee in a pan. Place over low heat, stirring, until chocolate and butter are melted. Cool slightly. Beat eggs in a mixer bowl and slowly beat in cooled chocolate mixture. Pour into an 8-inch springform pan. Bake in preheated 350 degree oven about 30 minutes, until cake cracks around sides. Cake will be soft in the center. Cool completely. Cover with foil and refrigerate overnight or up to 1 week. Loosen edge of cake with knife and remove sides of pan. Trim if necessary. Melt preserves or jelly and spread over top of cake. Return to refrigerator to set for 15 minutes. Whip cream with coffee granules until thick; fold in powdered sugar and vanilla. Top cake with whipped cream. Serves 10. NOTE: If 9-inch springform pan is used; increase recipe amounts by 1/2. Increased cooking time may be necessary.

Mississippi Mud Cake

2 sticks oleo

2 cups sugar

1/2 cup cocoa

4 eggs

1-1/3 cups flour

1-1/3 cups coconut

1 teaspoon vanilla

1 cup nuts, chopped

Cream oleo, sugar and cocoa; add eggs, beat well. Add flour and mix; add coconut, vanilla and nuts. Bake in 9x13" pan for 30 minutes. Cool cake for 30 minutes; pour 7-ounce jar of marshmallow creme over cake.

Frosting:

1 pound powdered sugar

4 tablespoons cocoa

1 stick oleo

1/4 cup evaporated milk

1 teaspoon vanilla

1/2 cup nuts

1/2 cup coconut

Mix all ingredients. Spread on cake.

Jannetta Duran

Peanut Butter Fudge Cake

1 cup butter or margarine
1/4 cup cocoa
1 cup water
1/2 cup buttermilk
2 eggs, well beaten
2 cups sugar
2 cups flour
1 teaspoon soda
1 teaspoon vanilla

Combine butter, cocoa, water, buttermilk and eggs in saucepan; stir constantly over low heat until it bubbles. In large bowl mix sugar, flour and soda; stir hot mixture into dry ingredients. Beat until smooth; add vanilla. Pour into a greased and floured 13x9x2" pan. Bake 25 minutes at 350 degrees or until puffed and firm to the touch in the center.

Frosting:

1-1/2 cups peanut butter
1-1/2 tablespoons peanut oil
1/4 cup cocoa
6 tablespoons buttermilk
1/2 cup butter or margarine
1 pound package powdered sugar
1 teaspoon vanilla

Mix peanut butter and oil in bowl until smooth; spread evenly over cooled cake. In saucepan heat butter, cocoa and buttermilk until bubbly. Place sugar in large bowl; beat in hot mixture until smooth. Stir in vanilla; spread evenly over peanut butter topping.

Sheath Cake

1 cup water
4 tablespoons cocoa
1/2 cup Crisco
1 stick oleo
1/2 cup buttermilk
1 teaspoon soda
2 eggs
2 cups sugar
2 cups flour
1 teaspoon cinnamon

Put four top ingredients in pan and bring to rapid boil. Pour over remaining ingredients; mix. Bake at 325 to 350 degrees until done.

Icing:

1 stick oleo
4 tablespoons cocoa
6 tablespoons sweetmilk

Bring to a boil. Add powdered sugar or marshmallow creme if you prefer until you reach right consistency. You can also add 1 cup chopped nuts if desired.

Irene Scroggins

"A bad habit is like a comfortable bed; easy to get into, but difficult to get out of."

31

Blackberry Jam Cake

2 cups sugar

1 cup butter

3 eggs

1 cup buttermilk

1 teaspoon soda

1 cup blackberry jam

1 cup pecans

1 cup raisins

1-1/2 cups coconut

3 cups flour

Cream sugar, butter and eggs. Add buttermilk and jam. Mix well. Mix soda and flour and add nuts, raisins and coconut. Mix well. Pour into greased and floured 10" tube pan. It will be thick. Bake at 350 degrees for 45 to 60 minutes.

Frosting:

2 cups sugar

1 cup butter

1-1/2 cups coconut

13-ounce can evaporated milk

1 cup nuts, chopped

Mix all together and cook over moderate heat until thick. About 7 minutes. This cake can be baked in loaf pans. Freezes really well.

"What the world calls a down right failure may actually be an upright man."

Punch Bowl Cake

1 box yellow cake mix

1 pint strawberries and juice

1 can crushed pineapple

2 or 3 sliced bananas

1 package vanilla instant pudding mix

2 packages Cool Whip

8-ounces cream cheese

1 cup pecans, chopped

1 can blueberry pie filling

1 large punch bowl

Bake cake as directed on package in three layers. Cool. Start with strawberries and juice in bottom of bowl. Crumble one layer of cake over strawberries. Spread crushed pineapple over cake. Crumble another layer of cake over the pineapple. Add sliced bananas on top then half of the prepared vanilla pudding (per package instructions). Add last layer of cake crumbled; top with remaining vanilla pudding mixture. Mix the Cool Whip and cream cheese. Place this on top of vanilla pudding. Sprinkle 1 cup chopped pecans over Cool Whip and cream cheese. Spread blueberry pie filling on top. Cover with more Cool Whip if desired. Refrigerate.

Floy McKaskle

Zucchini Squash Cake

3 cups sugar

1-1/2 cups Crisco oil

4 eggs

3 cups flour

1 teaspoon salt

1 teaspoon soda

2 teaspoons baking powder

1-1/2 teaspoons cinnamon

1 cup nuts

3 cups grated and peeled zucchini

Mix oil and sugar. Add eggs one at a time; add remainder of ingredients. Bake at 325 degrees for approximately 1 hour. Cool; ice with the following:

Icing:

3-ounces cream cheese

2 cups powdered sugar

1/4 stick oleo

1 teaspoon vanilla

Cream and ice cake.

Louise Vann

German Chocolate Cake

1 bar German chocolate

1/2 cup boiling water

1 cup butter

4 egg yolks

2 cups sugar

1 teaspoon vanilla

2-1/2 cups flour

1/2 teaspoon salt

1 teaspoon soda

1 cup buttermilk

4 egg whites, beaten stiff

Melt chocolate in boiling water. Cool. Cream butter and sugar until fluffy. Add egg yolks; beat. Add melted chocolate and vanilla. Mix dry ingredients; add alternately with buttermilk to chocolate mixture; beat well. Fold in egg whites. Pour in 3 greased and floured pans. Bake at 350 degrees for 30 to 40 minutes.

Icing:

1 cup evaporated milk

1 cup sugar

3 egg yolks

1/2 cup butter

1 teaspoon vanilla

Cook and stir over medium heat until thick. Add 1-1/3 cups coconut and 1 cup chopped pecans.

Joan McKaskle

Sorghum Molasses Cake

1 cup sugar

1 cup sorghum molasses

1 cup hot water

2 cups flour

1 teaspoon ginger

1 large egg

1 cup peanut oil

1 teaspoon (scant) soda

1 teaspoon salt

Add soda to hot water. Mix all ingredients in order given. Bake in 13x9x2" pan at 350 degrees for 30 to 35 minutes.

Esther Howard

7-Up Cake

1 pineapple cake mix
4 eggs
1 small box pineapple cream instant jello
3/4 cup oil
10-ounces 7-Up

Mix ingredients; bake at 350 degrees in two 9" pans. Cool; slice layers in half and frost.

Icing:
1-1/2 cups sugar
2 tablespoons flour
2 whole eggs
1 stick butter
1 large can crushed pineapple
1 cup coconut

Cook icing until thick. Add coconut; frost cake.

Hattie Hankins

Sock-It-To-Me-Cake

1 Duncan Hines butter cake mix
1 cup sour cream
1/3 cup Crisco oil
1/4 cup sugar
1/4 cup water
4 eggs

Filling:
2 tablespoons reserved cake mix
2 teaspoons cinnamon
2 tablespoons brown sugar
1 cup pecans, finely chopped

Combine filling ingredients; set aside. Combine all cake ingredients in bowl. Beat at high speed for 2 minutes. Pour 2/3 of batter in a prepared tube pan. Sprinkle filling ingredients over batter in pan. Spread remaining cake batter over filling. Bake at 375 degrees for 45-55 minutes. Cool 25 minutes; remove from pan.
Icing if desired: Blend 1 cup powdered sugar and 2 tablespoons milk. Drizzle over cake.

Barbara Smith

Hillbilly Cake

1 cup raisins
1 cup sugar
1/2 cup butter
1 cup water
1 teaspoon cinnamon
1/2 teaspoon allspice
2 cups flour
1 teaspoon baking soda
1/2 cup pecans

Boil together first 6 ingredients 2 minutes. Let cool; add to flour, baking soda, and pecans. Bake in a greased and floured 9x12" pan at 325 degrees for 20 minutes. Cool 10 minutes.

Icing:
1/2 cup melted butter
3 tablespoons evaporated milk
2/3 cup brown sugar
1/2 cup coconut
1 tablespoon flour
1 cup pecans

Mix. Spread icing; bake at 325 degrees for 20 minutes more.

Mrs. Laster

Jan's Fresh Apple Cake

1-1/2 cups Wesson oil

2 cups sugar

2 eggs, well beaten

3 cups flour

2 teaspoons vanilla

1 teaspoon soda

1 teaspoon salt

1 teaspoon baking powder

3 cups apples, chopped fine

1 cup nuts

Combine vanilla, oil, sugar and eggs; sift flour, salt, soda and baking powder then add to egg mixture. Add apples and nuts. Bake in a loaf layer for 40 to 75 minutes at 350 degrees.

Janis Mack

Pumpkin Cake

4 eggs

1-2/3 cups sugar

1 cup oil

16-ounce can pumpkin

Beat together until fluffy. Add:

2 cups flour

2 teaspoons baking powder

2 teaspoons cinnamon

1 teaspoon salt

1 teaspoon baking soda

Blend all ingredients. Bake 350 degrees 25 to 30 minutes.

Frosting:

1 small package cream cheese

1/2 cup margarine

1 teaspoon vanilla

2 cups powdered sugar

Blend and spread on cooled cake.

Patricia Neves

Milky Way Cake

8 Milky Way candy bars

2 sticks margarine

2 cups sugar

4 eggs, beaten

2-1/2 cups flour

1-1/4 cups buttermilk

1/2 teaspoon soda

1 cup pecans

Frosting:

2-1/2 cups sugar

1 cup evaporated milk

16-ounce package chocolate chips

1 stick butter

1 cup marshmallow creme

Melt 1 stick margarine and candy bars in double boiler. Cream sugar and 1 stick margarine and eggs, one at a time. Add flour, soda, salt and buttermilk. Blend well. Add melted candy and pecans. Bake at 350 degrees for 1 hour and 15 minutes. Cook sugar and milk; add marshmallow creme until a soft ball. Add chocolate chips and margarine. Stir and spread on cake.

Earthquake Cake

Grease and flour a 9x13 inch cake pan. Mix a German chocolate cake mix as directed.

1-1/2 cups pecans, chopped

1-1/2 cups coconut

Layer pecans and coconut in bottom of pan. Pour cake mix over this.

Mix:

8-ounces cream cheese

1 stick margarine

1 box powdered sugar

Pour over unbaked cake. Bake at 350 degrees for 45 to 60 minutes.

Heavenly Hash Cake

2 sticks oleo

4 tablespoons cocoa

2 cups sugar

4 eggs, beaten

1-1/2 cups flour

1 cup pecans, chopped

Miniature marshmallows

Icing:

1 stick oleo, melted

.4 tablespoons cocoa

4 tablespoons milk
(more is desired)

1 box powdered sugar

Melt oleo and cocoa in pan. Add sugar, eggs, flour and chopped pecans. Mix well and pour in 8x10-inch greased dish or pan. Bake 30 minutes at 350 degrees. Remove from oven and cover with miniature marshmallows. Return to oven to melt - about 3 minutes. Cool. Ice with melted oleo, cocoa, milk and powdered sugar mixed together.

Fresh Coconut Cake

1 package Duncan Hines Moist Deluxe Butter Recipe Golden Cake Mix

Bake cake as directed in two cake pans. Cool before icing.

Icing:

1 box powdered sugar

8-ounces cream cheese

1 stick margarine

1 small bag frozen fresh coconut, thawed

Mix first three ingredients well. Spread approximately 1/4 of the mixture between layers, topped with coconut. Spread remaining icing on top and around cake; top with rest of coconut.

Esther Howard

"Fill your memory with God's word, let it rule your heart and and direct your feet."

Candies & Sweet Treats

Fudge

Why bother making fudge, just place your order with the Pickle Barrel Fudge & Sweet Shop at Pickles Gap Village. Call 501-327-7708 or write for mail order brochure . . . we ship!

The Pickle Barrel Fudge & Sweet Shop is a fun place to work. Bonnie and Kerry welcome folks to sample our homemade fudge.

Fresh homemade fudge keeps our candy makers busy at Pickles Gap Village.

How to Tell. . . When Candy is Done

Use a good candy thermometer to take the guesswork out of candymaking. However, if you don't have one, follow the cold water test. Remove pan from heat; drop 1/2 teaspoon boiling syrup into a cup of very cold water. Form a ball with your fingers. Its firmness indicates temperature of syrup.

SOFT BALL...232 degrees to 240 degrees for fudge, pan nocha, and fondant. Syrup makes ball in cold water which can be picked up with fingers, but will not hold its shape.

FIRM BALL...242 degrees to 248 degrees for caramels and caramel corn. Syrup makes ball in cold water which holds its shape when picked up.

HARD BALL...250 degrees to 268 degrees for divinity and taffy. Ball in cold water is hard to the touch but still plastic.

SOFT CRACK...270 degrees to 290 degrees for toffee and butterscotch. Syrup forms hard but no brittle threads rather than a ball in cold water.

HARD CRACK... 300 degrees to 310 degrees for brittles, lollypops, taffy apples. Syrup forms brittle threads in cold water.

WEATHER ADJUSTMENT
On rainy or humid days, cook candy to 1 or 2 degrees higher temperature or slightly firmer stage than recipe directs.

ALTITUDE ADJUSTMENT...Subtract 1 degree for each 500 feet elevation above sea level when testing candy with a thermometer.

Pete Pleva

A big thanks to my Uncle Pete Pleva who contributed a lot of candy recipes to me. He is well known in Eugene, Oregon for his wonderful candy recipes. He enjoys making candy for his friends and relatives.

Pineapple Nut Fudge

3 cups sugar

2 tablespoons white corn syrup

1 cup crushed pineapple, packed in its own juice

2 teaspoons butter or margarine

3 cups miniature marshmallows

3 cups pecans

1 teaspoon vanilla

2 tablespoons lemon juice, must use real lemons

Few drops yellow food coloring

Cook first three ingredients until it makes a firm ball in cold water (244 degrees). Stir constantly while cooking. Remove from heat; add butter, marshmallows, nuts, vanilla, lemon juice and food coloring. Continue stirring constantly until candy becomes creamy and begins to stiffen. Spread on buttered platter; cut into squares.

Note: This candy has been in my family for over 50 years. My grandmother, Almedia Howard sent this to my Uncle Pete Pleva in Oregon several years ago and he makes this every Christmas for his friends. He added the lemon juice and food coloring to give a better flavor and texture.

Janis Mack

Uncle Pete's Crunch Bars

4 tablespoons Crisco shortening

3 cups crunched broken pieces of cheap saltine crackers

12-ounces semi-sweet chocolate chips

Melt chocolate chips and shortening over hot boiling water in double boiler. Remove from heat and add crackers. Blend well and press in a 11x18-inch glass platter lined with wax paper.

Pete Pleva

Yummy Peanut Butter Candy

6-ounce package butterscotch morsels

6-ounce package semi-sweet chocolate morsels

1/2 cup peanut butter

3 cups miniature marshmallows

1 cup salted peanuts

Melt first three ingredients together in double boiler over hot water until morsels melt and are well blended. Stir well. Remove from heat. Add 3 cups miniature marshmallows and 1 cup salted peanuts. Mix well. Spread in a foil lined 8" square pan. Chill until firm.

Pete Pleva

Uncle Pete's Hay Stacks

12-ounces butterscotch chips

3 cups chow mein noodles

1 cup Spanish peanuts

Dissolve butterscotch chips in top of double boiler over hot, not boilng water. Remove from heat. Blend in noodles and peanuts. Drop by spoonfuls onto wax paper. Chill and serve.

Pete Pleva

Sesame Taffy

1-1/2 cups sesame seeds

1/2 cup butter or margarine

1 cup white corn syrup

2 cups sugar

1/2 teaspoon salt

1 teaspoon vanilla

Spread sesame seeds on large baking sheets. Toast in 350 degree oven for 10 minutes or until light golden in color, stirring often. In a saucepan, melt margarine; stir in corn syrup and sugar. Cook and stir over high heat until temperature reaches 290 degrees. Remove from heat and stir in sesame seeds, salt and vanilla. Immediately pour on baking sheet to cool. Later break into pieces.

Pete Pleva

Chocolate Nut Puffs

1-1/2 cups chocolate chips

1/2 cup chunky style peanut butter

2 tablespoons butter

36 large marshmallows

1/2 cup nuts, chopped

In heavy saucepan combine chocolate chips, peanut butter and butter; heat, stirring occasionally until melted. Place marshmallows in 8-inch square pan; pour chocolate mixture over marshmallows; sprinkle with nuts. Chill until firm. Cut into squares. Makes about 36 puffs.

Pete Pleva

Tom's Orange Coconut Fantasy Fudge

3 cups white sugar

1-1/2 cubes margarine

1 small can evaporated milk

Dash salt

Boil above; stir constantly. Use only medium heat for 5-7 minutes. Remove from heat; stir in 12-ounces of chocolate chips, 7-ounce jar marshmallow creme, 1-1/2 teaspoons real orange extract; add 1 cup angel flake coconut. Stir quickly; pour on buttered cookie sheet or 9x13" cake pan. Let cool; cut into 1" squares. For variation, use vanilla extract and add 1 cup chopped walnuts.

Pete Pleva

Fabulous Fudge

2-1/4 cups sugar

3/4 cup evaporated milk

16 large marshmallow or
1 cup marshmallow creme

1/4 cup butter or margarine

1/4 teaspoon salt

6-ounce semi-sweet chocolate
chips (1 cup)

1 teaspoon vanilla

1 cup nuts, chopped (optional)

Mix sugar, evaporated milk,
marshmallows, butter or
margarine and salt in a heavy
medium saucepan. Cook,
stirring constantly, over
medium heat to an all over boil.
Boil and stir 5 minutes. Stir in
chocolate until completely
melted. Add vanilla and nuts.
Spread in buttered 8-inch
square pan. Cool. Cut into 30
pieces.   *Pete Pleva*

Apple Candy

2 cups cooked sieved tart apples

2 cups granulated sugar

1/8 teaspoon salt

2 to 3 tablespoons unflavored
gelatin

6 tablespoons cold water

1 cup walnuts, chopped

4 teaspoons lemon juice

Powdered sugar

Wash about 7-8 apples. Core
and cut unpeeled into small
pieces. Cook in
just enough water to
prevent from sticking to the
pan, until soft. Put through
sieve and measure. Combine
cooked apples, sugar and salt.
Cook until mixture becomes
thick, stirring constantly to
prevent scorching. Soak the
gelatin in the cold water to
soften it. Add to the hot apple
mixture, stirring until the
gelatin dissolves. Remove from
heat; add nuts and lemon juice
and pour into a well oiled
shallow pan. Cool, then
refrigerate. When candy has set,
cut into squares and roll in
powdered sugar. Makes about
65 pieces. (Note: Fresh cooked
or dried apricots may be
substituted for the apples.)
                         Pete Pleva

Double Peanut Clusters

1/2 cup peanut butter

1 cup semisweet chocolate bits

1 cup whole salted peanuts

Combine peanut butter and
chocolate pieces in top of
double boiler and place over hot
(not boiling) water until
chocolate melts. Stir until
blended. Add peanuts and stir
until well coated. Drop by
spoonfuls onto waxed paper
lined baking sheet. Chill until
set. Makes about 24 clusters.
                         Pete Pleva

Almond Butter Crunch

Note: A munchy candy sandwich, with a buttery crunchy center between two chocolate and nut layers. Makes 1 pound.

1-1/2 cups (12-ounces) whole blanched almonds, chopped

1 cup (2 sticks) butter or margarine

1-1/2 cups sugar

3 tablespoons light corn syrup

3 tablespoons water

8-ounces semisweet chocolate squares

Place chopped almonds on a cooky sheet; toast in 375 degree oven for 10 minutes or until lightly golden. Combine butter or margarine, sugar, corn syrup and water in a medium heavy saucepan. Cook over medium heat, stirring constantly to 300 degrees on a candy thermometer. (A teaspoon of syrup will separate into brittle threads when dropped in cold water.) Remove from heat; stir in 1 cup of the toasted almonds. Pour into a buttered 13x9x2-inch pan, spreading quickly and evenly; cool. Turn out onto wax paper. Melt chocolate squares in the top of a double boiler over hot water; remove from heat. Spread half the melted chocolate over top of candy; sprinkle with 1/4 cup nuts; let set for about 20 minutes; turn candy over; spread with remaining chocolate and sprinkle with remaining nuts. Let stand until set. Break into pieces. *Pete Pleva*

Cranberry White Fudge

4 cups sugar

1 cup milk

1 cup half and half cream

2 tablespoons light corn syrup

1/2 teaspoon salt

2 tablespoons butter or margarine

2 teaspoons vanilla extract

2 cups fresh or frozen-fresh cranberries

Combine sugar, milk, cream, corn syrup and salt. Cook to a boil until temperature on a candy thermometer registers 238 degrees, or until a soft ball forms when small amount of syrup is dropped into cold water. Cool until candy is lukewarm or 110 degrees. Beat in butter and vanilla. Beat until fudge becomes thick and holds its shape. Quickly stir in cranberries and spread into a buttered 8" square pan. Cool until firm and then cut into squares. (Note: To vary this basic white fudge, substitute 2/3 cup chopped nuts and 2/3 cup dried apricots for cranberries; or 1 cup chopped nuts and 1/2 cup chopped candied cherries.) *Pete Pleva*

Five-Minute Fudge

2/3 cup evaporated milk

1-2/3 cups sugar

1/2 teaspoon salt

1-1/2 cups diced marshmallows, about 16 medium

1-1/2 cups semisweet chocolate pieces

1 teaspoon vanilla

Combine evaporated milk, sugar and salt in saucepan over medium heat. Bring to boil; cook 4 to 5 minutes. Stir constantly. (Start timing when mixture starts to bubble around edges of pan.) Remove from heat. Add marshmallows, chocolate and vanilla. Stir vigorously for 1 minute or until marshmallows are completely melted and blended. Pour into 8-inch square buttered pan. Garnish with nuts if desired. Cool. Cut into squares.

For Peppermint Fudge: Sprinkle 1/4 cup coarsely broken peppermint stick candy over top of fudge in pan.

For Upside Down Coconut Fudge: Spread 1 cup flaked coconut on bottom of buttered 8-inch square and top with fudge.

For Nut Fudge: Add 1/2 cup chopped walnuts, pecans or peanuts to fudge mixture before pouring in pan. *Pete Pleva*

Old-Fashioned Chocolate Fudge

What is a candy shop without marvelous, melt-in-your-mouth chocolate fudge. Makes 2 pounds.

1-1/2 cups milk

4 squares unsweetened chocolate, 4-ounces

4 cups sugar

3 tablespoons light corn syrup

1/4 teaspoon salt

3 tablespoons butter or margarine

1-1/2 teaspoons vanilla

Combine milk and chocolate in medium size heavy saucepan; cook over low heat until chocolate is melted. Add sugar, corn syrup and salt; cook, stirring constantly to boiling. Cook without stirring to 234 degrees on a candy thermometer. (To soft ball stage.) Remove from heat at once. Add vanilla and butter, but do not stir in. Leave thermometer in pan while fudge is cooling. Let mixture cool to 110 degrees. When cool enough, you can rest bottom of pan comfortably on your hand. Beat with wooden spoon until mixture thickens and just begins to lose its gloss. Mixture will lighten in color as you beat, about 15 minutes. Spread in buttered 8x8x2"pan. Cool; cut into squares.

Pete Pleva

42

Butterscotch Fudge

1 cup walnuts, chopped fine

7-ounce jar marshmallow cream

1-1/2 cups sugar

2/3 cup evaporated milk

1/4 cup butter (1/2 stick)

1/4 teaspoon salt

12-ounce package butterscotch flavored morsels (2 cups)

1 teaspoon orange extract

1 teaspoon grated orange rind

Line 8-inch square pan with foil. Spread 1/2 cup walnuts evenly on bottom of pan; set aside. In heavy gauge saucepan, combine marshmallow cream, sugar, evaporated milk, butter and salt. Bring to full rolling boil over moderate heat, stirring constantly. Boil 5 minutes, stirring constantly. Remove from heat. Add butterscotch morsels; stir until morsels are melted and mixture is smooth. Stir in extract and rind. Pour into prepared pan. Sprinkle remaining 1/2 cup walnuts on top. Chill until firm (about 2 hours). Makes about 2-1/3 lbs.

Pete Pleva

Mocha Peanut Clusters

1/3 cup butter or margarine

6-ounce package semisweet chocolate pieces

4-ounce package full-sized marshmallows (16)

1 teaspoon instant coffee powder or granules

2 cups chopped salted peanuts

Place butter, chocolate pieces and marshmallows in the top of a double boiler over simmering water. Cook, stirring occasionally, until chocolate and marshmallows are melted; stir in instant coffee. Remove from heat; stir in peanuts. Line two cookie sheets with wax paper. Drop rounded teaspoonfuls of the peanut mixture onto the wax paper. Chill in refrigerator until hard. Makes 3 dozen clusters.

Pete Pleva

Crunchy Chews

3/4 cup dark corn syrup

3/4 cup sugar

3/4 cup creamy or chunk style peanut butter

3/4 cup broken nuts

4-1/2 cups corn flakes

Combine corn syrup and sugar in large saucepan. Bring to full boil, stirring constantly. Remove from heat. Quickly stir in peanut butter. Add nuts and cereal, stirring to coat evenly. Turn into greased 13x9-inch pan. Cool. Cut into squares. Makes 4-1/2 dozen (1-1/2 inch) squares.

Pete Pleva

43

Molasses Coconut Chews

1-1/4 cups sugar

2/3 cup light corn syrup

1/3 cup molasses

2 tablespoons butter or margarine

3 cans (4-ounces each) shredded coconut - about 4 cups

Combine sugar, corn syrup, molasses and butter in a large saucepan. Cook, stirring until sugar dissolves. Cover pan for 1 minute to allow the steam to wash down the sugar crystals that cling to side of pan; or wipe down the crystals with a damp cloth. Uncover pan; insert candy thermometer. Cook without stirring until candy thermometer reaches 253 degrees (hard ball stage, where syrup when dropped in very cold water forms a ball in the fingers that is hard enough to hold a shape, yet still plastic.) Remove from heat; stir in the coconut. Pour mixture into a well-buttered 13x9x2-inch pan. Cool until lukewarm or comfortable to handle. Form candy into 1/2-inch balls, then cool completely before coating with granulated sugar or chocolate. **For sugar coating:** Roll cooled balls in granulated sugar. **For chocolate coating:** Melt a 12-ounce package of semi-sweet chocolate pieces in top of double boiler over hot - not boiling - water. Dip each coconut ball in the chocolate. Lift out with a fork; tap off excess chocolate on edge of pan. Cool on wax paper until chocolate is firm. Store 2 to 3 weeks in refrigerator or in tightly covered container with foil or plastic wrap between layers in a cool dry place. Makes 2-1/2 pounds with chocolate or 2-1/4 pounds without.

Pete Pleva

Quick Peanut Butter Fudge

1/3 cup margarine

1/2 cup light corn syrup

3/4 cup creamy or chunk style peanut butter

1 teaspoon vanilla

1/2 teaspoon salt

1 pound powdered sugar, sifted

3/4 cup nuts, chopped

Blend margarine, corn syrup, peanut butter, vanilla and salt in large mixing bowl. Stir in powdered sugar gradually. Turn onto board and knead until well blended and smooth. Add nuts gradually, pressing and kneading into candy. Press out with hands or rolling pin into squares 1/2-inch thick. Cut into serving pieces. Makes about 2 pounds.

Pete Pleva

Peanut Butter Fudge

2 cups sugar

1/4 cup light corn syrup

1/2 cup milk

1/4 teaspoon salt

2 tablespoons butter or margarine

1 teaspoon vanilla

1 cup crunchy or smooth peanut butter

1/2 cup peanuts, chopped fine (optional)

Combine sugar, corn syrup, milk and salt in a medium saucepan. Cook over low heat; stir constantly until sugar dissolves. Cover pan for 1 minute to allow the steam to wash down the sugar crystals that cling to the side of pan, or wipe down the crystals with a damp cloth. Uncover pan; insert candy thermometer. Cook without stirring until candy thermometer reaches 236 degrees (soft ball stage). Remove from heat. Add butter. Cool syrup until lukewarm (110 degrees). Add vanilla, peanut butter and nuts. Beat until candy begins to thicken and loses its high gloss. Turn immediately into a buttered 8x8x2-inch pan. Score with a sharp knife into small squares; cool. When completely cool, cut squares all the way through. Store 2 to 3 weeks in tightly covered container with foil or plastic wrap between layers. Makes about 2 pounds. A creamy and peanutty treat for the whole family!

Pete Pleva

Double-Decker Fudge

4-1/2 cups sugar

7-ounce jar marshmallow creme

2 (6-ounce) cans evaporated milk(1-1/3 cups)

1/2 cup butter or margarine

Dash salt

6-ounce package (1 cup) semi-sweet chocolate pieces

6-ounce package (1 cup) butterscotch pieces

In 3-quart saucepan, combine sugar, marshmallow creme, evaporated milk, butter or margarine, and salt. Cook and stir over medium heat till mixture boils. Boil gently, stirring frequently for 5 minutes. Divide mixture in half. To one half (about 3 cups) add chocolate pieces; stir till melted and blended. Pour into buttered 13x9x2-inch pan. To remaining half of marshmallow mixture, add the butterscotch pieces. Beat until smooth. Pour over chocolate layer; cool. Cut in pieces. If desired, drizzle with melted chocolate!

Pete Pleva

Cherry Vanilla Fudge

3 cups sugar

1/2 teaspoon salt

1 cup light cream

1/2 cup milk

1/4 cup light corn syrup

2 tablespoons butter or margarine

2 teaspoons vanilla

1 cup red and green candied cherries, cut in quarters

Combine sugar, salt, cream, milk, corn syrup and butter in a large heavy saucepan. Cook over medium heat, stirring constantly until mixture comes to boiling. Continue cooking, stirring occasionally, until candy thermometer reaches 238 degrees (soft ball stage). Remove from heat, leaving thermometer in the saucepan. Cool to 100 degrees. Add vanilla. Beat briskly until fudge thickens and begins to lose its gloss. Stir in cherries. Pour into buttered 8-inch square pan. Cool; cut into squares when firm. Note: This vanilla fudge is full of bright bits of candied cherries. So colorful, delicious and easy! Makes 1-3/4 pounds.

Pete Pleva

Jesus died among sinners, that we might dwell among saints."

Peanut Brittle

2 cups roasted, salted Spanish peanuts

2 cups brown sugar, firmly packed

1/2 cup water

3/4 cup light corn syrup

2 tablespoons butter

1/2 teaspoon vanilla

1 teaspoon soda (free from lumps)

Spread peanuts in baking pan and set in 200 degree oven. In 3-quart saucepan mix sugar, water and syrup. Cook over medium heat to 295 degrees (hard-crack stage) stirring constantly until sugar dissolves, then often to prevent burning. Stir in butter, then hot peanuts and vanilla. Remove from heat; at once add soda, stirring rapidly until light and foamy. Quickly pour onto well-oiled marble slab or 2 large cookie sheets, spreading thin. Soon as brittle begins to set, loosen and flip over. Stretch as thin as possible. Let cool, then break into pieces. Store tightly covered. Makes about 2 pounds. This is full of flavor and easy to make!

Pete Pleva

Using your bible as a road map keeps you off the detours of sin."

46

Divinity Drops

2-1/2 cups sugar
3/4 cup water
1/2 cup light corn syrup
1/8 teaspoon salt
2 egg whites
1/2 teaspoon vanilla
1/8 teaspoon orange extract
Walnut or pecan halves or candied cherries

Combine sugar, water, syrup and salt in 2-quart saucepan. Bring to boil over medium heat, stirring constantly. Boil gently, without stirring, until temperature reaches 255 degrees, or until a small amount of mixture dropped into very cold water forms a ball which is hard enough to hold its shape, yet plastic. Meanwhile, beat egg whites in large bowl with electric mixer until stiff peaks form when beater is raised. Beating constantly at high speed, pour hot syrup in fine stream over egg whites. Beat in vanilla and orange extract. Continue beating until mixture begins to lose its gloss and a small amount of mixture holds its shape when dropped from spoon. (If mixture becomes too stiff for mixer, beat with wooden spoon.) Drop by teaspoonfuls onto waxed paper. Insert a nut half or candied cherry into center of each. Let stand until set. Makes about 1 pound.

Pete Pleva

Fondant

1/3 cup margarine
1/3 cup light corn syrup
1 teaspoon vanilla
1/2 teaspoon salt
1 pound powdered sugar, sifted

Blend margarine, syrup, vanilla and salt. Add powdered sugar all at once and mix in, first with spoon, then kneading with hands. Turn out onto board and knead until mixture is well blended and smooth. Store in cool place. Shape as desired. Makes 1-1/3 pounds.

Bon Bons: Flavor and tint fondant as desired. Shape into balls with nut piece in center. Roll in colored or white sugar or in chocolate or multicolor sprinkles for decorating.

Filled Fruit or Nuts: Fill center of pitted prunes, dates or apricots with fondant or place fondant between nut halves. Roll in sugar.

Pete Pleva

Almond Butter Crunch Wheels

1 cup blanched slivered almonds (or peanuts)

1/2 cup butter or margarine

1/2 cup sugar

1 tablespoon light corn syrup

Line bottom and sides of 8 or 9-inch cake pan with foil. Butter the foil; set aside. Combine almonds, butter, sugar and syrup in skillet. Bring to a boil over medium heat, stirring constantly until mixture turns golden brown about 5 or 6 minutes. Working quickly, spread candy in pan. Cool about 15 minutes or until firm. Remove candy from pan by lifting edges of foil. Peel off the foil. Cool thoroughly. Candy may be presented as a disk or broken into pieces. Makes about 3/4 pound.

Grandmother Howard

Divinity Candy

2-3/4 cups sugar

3/4 cup white syrup

3/4 cup water

2 egg whites

1 teaspoon vanilla

3/4 cut nuts

Mix sugar, water and syrup. Cook until it spins thread or forms soft ball in cold water. Beat egg whites until stiff. Pour 3/4 mixture over stiff egg whites. Cook the rest until it is firm in water. Then pour into egg whites and beat until you can drop off spoon. Pour into pan lined with waxed paper. (To add flavor and color, add a small jar of drained maraschino cherries.)

Esther Howard

Peanut Butter Fudge

1 stick oleo

1 box brown sugar

1 box powdered sugar

3/4 cup Pet milk

1 cup peanut butter

1 cup nuts, chopped

1 teaspoon vanilla

Melt oleo in heavy skillet. Add brown sugar and Pet milk and bring to boil, stirring constantly. Boil 2 minutes. Continue to stir constantly. Add peanut butter, vanilla and nuts. Gradually stir in powdered sugar and beat well. Pat into buttered platter.

Ruth Poe

Thanks to one of my favorite cousins, Ruth Poe and her daughter-in-law, Beckie Poe for sharing some great recipes!!

Non-Sticking Caramel Corn

2 cups brown sugar

3/4 cup margarine

1/2 teaspoon cream of tartar

1/2 teaspoon salt

1/2 cup light corn syrup

1 teaspoon soda

7 cups popped corn

1 cup raw peanuts

Boil brown sugar, margarine, cream of tartar, salt and corn syrup together for five minutes. Remove from heat and add soda, stirring well. Pour over corn and peanuts that have been mixed together; coat well. Spread coated corn on cookie sheet and bake at 200 degrees for one hour, stirring every 15 minutes. Remove from oven and stir several times as mixture cools, separating the corn and peanuts into small portions. Store in covered cans. This makes a good mailable treat for college students!

Becky Poe

Fudge

2 cups white sugar

2/3 cup evaporated milk

1/2 cup butter or margarine

12 large marshmallows

1 tablespoon instant coffee (Folger's works best)

Pinch salt

6-ounce package white chocolate flavored baking bar, chopped

1 cup pecans, chopped

1 teaspoon vanilla

Combine first six ingredients. Cook over medium-low heat stirring constantly until it comes to a boil. Cover, simmer 5 to 6 minutes. Remove from heat. Add chocolate and remaining ingredients. Stir until it melts. Spoon into buttered 8-inch square pan. Cool.

Quick Party Mints

1 pound powdered sugar, sifted

Desired food coloring

3-ounce package cream cheese at room temperature

Desired flavoring

Mash cream cheese; add sugar gradually until all sugar is used. This makes a stiff dough. Make into marble size balls and roll in granulated sugar. Press into candy mold or place on wax paper and press with a design. Note: Let dry for 1 hour and keep in tight container.

Val's Chocolate Oatmeal Balls

1 box powdered sugar

1 cup peanut butter

1 cup coconut

1/2 cup instant oatmeal

1 teaspoon vanilla

2 sticks margarine

Stir, mixing well and shape into balls (approximately 40) and chill. Melt 1/2 bar paraffin (1/8 pound) and 1 cup chocolate chips in double boiler. Dip and drain on wax paper.

Val Gifford

Chocolate Covered Cherries

8 tablespoons melted butter

6 tablespoons corn syrup

1 can condensed milk

1 teaspoon vanilla

1 large jar maraschino cherries (drained)

2-1/2 to 3 pounds powdered sugar

Blend all ingredients (except cherries) together. Knead and form into balls with a cherry in the middle of each ball. Set in freezer for about an hour. Dip into the following mixture and drop onto wax paper.

Dip:

1 block paraffin wax

12-ounce package milk chocolate chips

Melt together in top of a double boiler. Dip the cold cherry balls into the dip.

Janis Mack

D-Easy Fudge

2 sticks margarine

12-ounces semisweet chocolate chips

2 eggs, beaten until stiff

1-pound powdered sugar

1 tablespoon vanilla

1 to 1-1/2 cups walnuts

Melt margarine and chocolate chips together on low heat. Beat eggs; add sugar and beat till creamy. Add vanilla; add walnuts. Lightly grease 9x12-inch pan with butter and pour mixture into pan. Refrigerate to set.

Peanut Butter Balls

Mix together:

1 pound powdered sugar

3 cups Rice Krispies

1/2 cup margarine

2 cups crunchy peanut butter

Roll into balls.
Melt together:

6-ounces chocolate chips

1/8-pound paraffin

Dip balls into the paraffin.

Peanut Butter Fudge

4 cups sugar
1 can evaporated milk
1 stick butter
1 jar marshmallow creme
2 cups crunchy peanut butter

Bring sugar, milk and butter to a boil. Cook to medium soft ball stage stirring frequently. Remove from heat; add creme and peanut butter. Stir until creme and peanut butter are thoroughly blended and the candy loses its gloss. Pour into 13x9-inch pan. Let cool and cut.

Diana Hensley

Chocolate Icebox Treat

8-ounce box Bakers semi-sweet chocolate
2 sticks butter or margarine
5 tablespoons sugar
3 large eggs
1 teaspoon vanilla
12 shortcakes or 3 packages of lady fingers

In heavy saucepan, melt chocolate, butter and sugar over low heat. Stir until dissolved. Cool (cold). Put mixture in large mixing bowl, beat in eggs, one at a time. Beat on high speed for 15 minutes. Add vanilla. Split shortcakes in thirds and line the bottom of a

7-1/2x 13-inch glass dish. Use half of the mixture of chocolate on top of cakes; put another layer of the cakes on top and finish it off with remaining chocolate. Refrigerate until firm. A chocolate lover's dream!

Easy Peanut Butter Fudge

12-ounces peanut butter flavored chips
14-ounce can sweetened condensed milk
1/4 cup margarine
1/2 cup peanuts, chopped
6-ounce package semisweet chocolate morsels

In a large saucepan, melt peanut butter chips, 1 cup sweetened condensed milk and 2 tablespoons margarine. Stir occasionally. Remove from heat. Stir in peanuts. Spread mixture into waxed paper lined 8" square pan. In a small saucepan melt the chocolate morsels, remaining sweetened condensed milk and margarine. Spread chocolate mixture on top of peanut butter mixture. Chill 2 hours or until firm. Turn fudge onto cutting board and peel off waxed paper. Cut into squares and tightly cover any leftovers. Makes about 2 pounds.

Jean Young

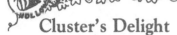

Cluster's Delight

11-1/2 ounces vanilla chips

1-1/2 cups Granola
(Quaker Oats)

In a double boiler, melt the vanilla chips over hot, but not boiling water. Remove from fire; add Granola. Blend well using two spoons. Drop by teaspoonful onto waxed paper. Takes around 20 minutes to set. Place in container. . . will freeze well!

Pete Pleva

Vanilla Clusters

11-1/2 ounces vanilla chips

1-1/2 cups nuts (chopped pecans or walnuts)

Melt the vanilla chips in double boiler over hot but not boiling water. Remove from heat. Add nuts and blend well. Drop by teaspoonful onto waxed paper. Candy will be set in 20 minutes or less. Will yield 4 dozen pieces. Store in container. . .very good to freeze.

Pete Pleva

"Reputation is what men think you are. Character is what God knows you are."

Pecan Roll

Ingredients for inside:

2 cups sugar

1/2 cup light corn syrup

1/2 cup water

2 egg whites

1 teaspoon vanilla

Ingredients for Caramel Covering:

1 cup sugar

1/2 cup brown sugar

1/2 cup light corn syrup

1/2 cup cream

1 cup milk

1/4 cup butter or oleo

Cook sugar, syrup and water until hard crack stage (or spins thread when poured from spoon). Pour slowly over 2 egg whites that have been beaten until stiff. Add vanilla. Continue to beat until stiff and cool enough to handle. Form into 1x6 or 8" long rolls, on buttered waxed paper. Cook caramel ingredients until they form a firm ball; cool slightly. While still quite warm, dip roll of divinity in caramel and roll in nuts. Divinity roll should be very cold before dipping. You will need about 5 cups of coarsely chopped nuts. Makes 6 to 8 rolls.

Sour Cream Glazed Pecans

To toast, spread a single layer of nuts in a shallow pan. Bake at 325 degrees for 12-15 minutes.

1-1/2 cups sugar

1/2 cup dairy sour cream

1-1/2 teaspoons vanilla

3 cups toasted pecan halves

Combine sugar and sour cream in a heavy 1-1/2 to 2-quart saucepan. Cook over medium-high heat to boiling, stirring constantly. Reduce heat to medium and cook about 5 minutes more, stirring constantly. Remove from heat. Stir in vanilla. Add pecans and stir to coat well. Spread pecans onto waxed paper and quickly separate pecan halves into clusters with two buttered forks. Cool and store, covered in the refrigerator for up to 1 month, or in the freezer for up to 6 months. Makes 5 cups.

Jan Barrow

Glazed Pecans

1 pound shelled pecans

1/2 cup margarine

1/4 cup light corn syrup

Salt

Spread pecans evenly in an 8-1/2x13-inch aluminum pan. Scatter margarine in pats over nuts. Drizzle corn syrup over nuts. Roast in slow oven 250 to 300 degrees, stirring occasion-ally until slightly browned (about one hour). Add extra margarine if spoon becomes sticky when stirring. Line counter with brown paper; spread roasted nuts on paper; salt generously, tossing nuts to insure all are covered.

Sugared Pecans

2 pounds pecan halves

4 egg whites

2 cups sugar

1 pinch salt

3/4 cup butter

Beat egg whites; add salt and sugar. Fold in pecans. Melt butter; pour over pecan mixture. Mix well. Spread on cookie sheet with edges. Bake at 350 degrees for 30-45 minutes (golden brown) stir every 10 minutes. Store in airtight container.

Charlotte Roberts

Praline Pecan Crunch

16-ounce package Quaker Oat Squares cereal (8 cups)

2 cups pecan pieces

1/2 cup light corn syrup

1/2 cup firmly packed brown sugar

1/4 cup margarine (1/2 stick)

1 teaspoon vanilla

(Continued on next page)

(Continued from previous page)
1/2 teaspoon baking soda

Heat oven to 250 degrees. Combine cereal and pecans in 13x9-inch pan; set aside. Combine syrup, sugar and margarine in 2-cup microwaveable bowl. Microwave on high 1-1/2 minutes; stir. Microwave on high 1/2 to 1-1/2 minutes more or until boiling. Stir in vanilla and baking soda; pour over cereal mixture. Stir to coat evenly. Bake 1 hour; stirring every 20 minutes. Spread on baking sheet to cool; break into pieces. Makes 10 cups.

Jan Barrow

Potato Candy

2 small potatoes, baked
1-1/2 to 2 boxes powdered sugar
1 teaspoon vanilla flavoring
Crunchy peanut butter

Peel potatoes; mash in large mixing bowl. Gradually add flavoring and sugar until mixture is like dough; roll out on waxed paper. Spread generously with peanut butter; roll into a log. Chill for several hours or overnight. Slice and store in the refrigerator. Rolls may be frozen. Makes 50-60 pieces.

"Don't pretend to be what you don't intend to be."

Shoestring Potato Candy

2 (6-ounce) packages butterscotch chips
1 cup nuts, chopped
3 tablespoons peanut butter
14-ounce can shoestring potatoes

Melt butterscotch chips and peanut butter. Pour over potatoes and nuts. Mix gently. Drop onto waxed paper covered cookie sheet by teaspoon. Place in freezer to set. Remove from freezer when firm.

Fat-Free Grape-Nut Divinity

4 cups sugar
1/2 cup water
1 cup light corn syrup
3 egg whites
1 teaspoon vanilla
1 cup Grape-Nuts cereal

Put first 3 ingredients in saucepan; cook until soft ball. Take 1/3 of mixture; pour over stiffly beaten egg whites; beat constantly. Place the rest of syrup back on the fire; cook to a firm ball. Pour over the first part; continue beating. Add vanilla. When it begins to thicken, add cereal; drop by teaspoons onto waxed paper, sprayed with non-fat spray.

Cookies & Cream

Treat yourself to some ice cream or fudge at the Pickle Barrel Fudge & Sweet Shop at Pickles Gap Village, Conway, Arkansas.

WARNING: Raw eggs used in making homemade ice cream could be harmful to your health. Best to use egg substitute or cook egg mixture if possible. Check the recipe.
(See page 119 for more information.)

What a fun place for kids. The Pickle Barrel Fudge & Sweet Shop is everyone's favorite! (Especially our grand children!)

Low-Fat Old Fashion Oatmeal Cookies

1 cup sugar
1 cup brown sugar
1-1/2 cups liquid Butter Buds
2-1/2 to 3 cups flour
1 cup raisins (boiled)
1 tablespoon raisin water
1 teaspoon allspice
1 teaspoon cinnamon
2 Egg Beaters
1 cup quick oat oatmeal
1 teaspoon soda
1 tablespoon vanilla
1 teaspoon nutmeg
1 cup Grape Nuts cereal

Cover raisins with water and boil until they are puffed up. Cream together sugars and Butter Buds. Add Egg Beaters, oatmeal, flour, raisins, and soda mixed with the raisin water. Next add vanilla, spices, and Grape-Nuts. Chill dough 30 minutes. Drop by spoonfuls on cookie sheet sprayed with non-fat cooking spray. Bake 17-20 minutes at 325 degrees. Makes 6 dozen cookies.

"People who tell little white lies soon go color blind."

Low-Fat So Good Snickerdoodles

1 cup Smart Beat margarine
2-1/2 cups powdered sugar
1 tablespoon vanilla
2 teaspoons almond extract
2 Egg Beaters
2-1/2 to 3 cups self-rising flour
3 tablespoons granulated sugar
1 tablespoon ground cinnamon

Cream together margarine, powdered sugar, vanilla, almond and Egg Beaters until smooth. Add flour and blend thoroughly. Chill dough one hour. On a small plate mix together granulated sugar and cinnamon. Drop dough by spoonful into the cinnamon-sugar mixture. The dough will be very sticky. Sprinkle cinnamon-sugar mixture over dough until it is coated enough to roll. Next place the coated balls on a cookie sheet that has been sprayed with Pam Spray. Bake at 375 degrees for 8 to 10 minutes. Makes 5 dozen cookies.

"People who fly into a rage always make a bad landing."

Low-Fat Chocolate Cake Bars

1 cup applesauce

3/4 cup buttermilk

1 cup pineapple juice

3 tablespoons cocoa

2 cups flour

1 teaspoon cinnamon

1/2 cup Hershey's Chocolate Syrup

2 cups sugar

2 Egg Beaters

1 teaspoon baking soda

1/2 cup buttermilk

Frosting:

2 egg whites

1/3 cup water

1-1/2 cups sugar

1/2 teaspoon cream of tartar

1 tablespoon light corn syrup

3/4 cup marshmallow creme or 16 marshmallows

4 tablespoons cocoa

1/2 cup Grape-Nuts cereal, optional

Preheat oven to 350 degrees. Spray a 13x9-inch cake pan with a non-fat cooking spray. In a medium saucepan, simmer pineapple juice until it is reduced in volume to 1/2 cup. Meanwhile, in a medium bowl, combine applesauce, butter-milk, and cocoa powder. Set aside. In large bowl, combine flour, cinnamon and sugar; set aside. When pineapple juice is reduced, add applesauce mixture to saucepan. Increase heat to medium, and stir until mixture boils. Pour heated mixture into flour mixture, and mix well with a spoon. Cool to lukewarm. Add Egg Beaters to lukewarm batter, and mix well. Dissolve baking soda in 1/2 cup buttermilk. Add to batter and stir only until mixed; add Hershey's syrup; do not overstir. Pour into pan. Bake for 35-45 minutes, until inserted toothpick comes out clean.

Frosting:

Combine egg whites, sugar, cream of tartar, syrup and water in top of a double boiler. Place over boiling water; beat with a rotary beater until stiff peaks form, scraping pan occasionally. Remove from heat. Add sifted cocoa and marshmallow creme and continue beating until it is of spreading consistency. Spread over cooled cake. Sprinkle Grape-Nuts cereal over top if desired. Makes 24 bars.

"The measure of life is not its duration, but its donation."

Esther's Cookies

2 cups flour

1-1/4 cups sugar

1 cup Crisco

2 eggs

1 teaspoon vanilla

1 teaspoon salt

Mix sugar and eggs together. Add Crisco to dry ingredients; mix well. Add to eggs and sugar mixture; mix well. Chill for an hour; roll out on floured surface; cut with cookie cutter and place on greased cookie sheet. Bake approximately 10 minutes in a 350 degree oven or until slightly brown. *These are good with a fudge type filling between 2 cooked cookies. . . Sandwich cookie if you like!*

Esther Howard

Chewy Bar Cookies

1/2 cup butter or margarine

1 cup firmly packed light brown sugar

1 cup firmly packed dark brown sugar

2 eggs

1-1/2 cups all purpose flour

1-1/2 teaspoons baking powder

1/2 teaspoon salt

1 cup nuts, chopped

1 teaspoon vanilla extract

Blend butter and sugars. Do not mix too much if a chewy cookie is desired. Add eggs and beat well. Combine flour, baking powder and salt; add to creamed mixture. Add vanilla extract and nuts. Spread in a greased 13x9x2-inch pan. Bake at 325 degrees for 30 minutes. Cut into bars while still warm, but leave in pan until cold. Makes 4 dozen. *My mother would bake these cookies and send them to me while I was at church camp in the summer. I found it was easy to make friends when these cookies arrived.*

Becky Poe

Crunchy Peanut Butter Treats

3/4 cup corn syrup (white)

3/4 cup sugar

1 cup peanut butter (smooth or crunchy

3 cups corn flakes

Mix syrup and sugar in medium sized saucepan and heat until it bubbles. Remove immediately and add peanut butter mixing until well blended. Mix in corn flakes gradually. Drop by tablespoonfuls on to foil. Let cool.

Bill Ellis

"Little things become great things when done in God's power."

57

Reese's Cookies

1 cup Butter Flavored Crisco
1 cup sugar
1/2 cup packed light brown sugar
1 teaspoon vanilla
2 eggs
2 cups unsifted all purpose flour
1 teaspoon baking soda
1 cup Reese's Peanut Butter chips
1 cup Hershey's Chocolate chips

Cream shortening, sugar, brown sugar and vanilla until light and fluffy. Add eggs; beat well. Combine four and baking soda and blend into creamed mixture. Stir in chips. Drop by teaspoonfuls onto ungreased cookie sheet. Bake at 350 degrees for 10-12 minutes or unti lightly browned. Cool slightly and remove from cookie sheet.

Jean Young

Dream Bars

Dough:
1/3 cup soft shortening
1/2 cup brown sugar
2 tablespoons evaporated milk
1 cup sifted flour

Filling:
1 egg
1 cup brown sugar, firmly packed

1/4 teaspoon salt
1 teaspoon baking powder
3 tablespoons evaporated milk
1 teaspoon vanilla
4-ounce can shredded coconut
6-ounce package chocolate pieces
1/2 cup pecans, chopped
2 tablespoons flour

Mix shortening, 1/2 cup brown sugar and 2 tablespoons evaporated milk until light and fluffy. Gradually mix in flour. Press dough evenly over the bottom of a greased 13x9x1-1/2" pan. Bake in 325 degree oven 15 minutes. Beat egg until foamy in medium bowl. Beat in brown sugar, salt, baking powder, evaporated milk and vanilla. Stir in coconut, chocolate pieces, nuts and flour. Using two forks, spread on baked dough. Bake 30 minutes or until top is brown. Cut into 32 bars.

Uncle Pete Pleva

Coffee Toffee Bars

Bars:

1 cup butter or margarine

1 cup brown sugar

1 teaspoon almond flavoring

1-2 teaspoons instant coffee granules

2-1/4 cups flour

1/2 teaspoon baking powder

1/4 teaspoon salt

6-ounce package chocolate chips

1/2 cup nuts, chopped

Combine butter, sugar and flavoring. Add dry ingredients, chips and nuts. Press into greased 13x9-inch pan and bake at 350 degrees for 30-35 minutes. While warm add glaze.

Glaze:

1 tablespoon butter or margarine, softened

3/4 cup powdered sugar

1/3 teaspoon almond flavoring

2 tablespoons milk

Mix all ingredients until smooth. Glaze warm bars. Cut into small bars. Makes 2 dozen.

"Contentment is not found in having everything, but being satisfied with everything."

Chocolate White Treasure Brownies

1 cup all-purpose flour

1/4 teaspoon baking soda

1/4 teaspoon salt

3/4 cup sugar

1/3 cup butter

2 tablespoons water

6-ounce package semi-sweet chocolate morsels (1 cup) or 3 bars (6-ounces) semi-sweet chocolate baking bars

1 teaspoon vanilla extract

2 eggs

10-ounce package (1-1/2 cups) Nestlé Premier White Treasures baking pieces

Preheat oven to 325 degrees. In small bowl, combine flour, baking soda and salt; set aside. In small saucepan over medium heat, combine sugar, butter and water. Bring just to a boil; remove from heat. Add semi-sweet chocolate bits and vanilla extract. Stir until chocolate melts and mixture is smooth. Transfer to large bowl. Add eggs, one at a time, beating well after each addition. Gradually blend in flour mixture. Stir in White Treasures baking pieces. Spread into greased 9-inch baking pan. Bake 30 to 35 minutes. Cool completely. Cut into 2" squares. Makes 16 squares. **Uncle Pete Pleva**

Nutty Blonde Brownies

1/2 cup butter, softened
1 cup firmly packed brown sugar
1 egg
1 teaspoon vanilla
1 cup all-purpose flour
1/4 teaspoon soda
1/4 teaspoon salt
1/2 to 1 cup chocolate chips
1/2 cup pecans

Cream butter. Gradually add brown sugar and beat well. Add egg and vanilla. Beat well. Combine flour, soda, and salt and add to cream mixture. Mix and stir in chocolate morsels and pecans. Spread into pan and bake at 350 degrees for 20 to 25 minutes. Cool and cut into squares. Makes about 3 dozen 1-1/2-inch squares. Don't overbake!

Christine Garrison

Coffee-Date Squares

1 cup butter or margarine (2 sticks), melted
1 cup brown sugar firmly packed
1/2 cup triple-strength coffee
2 cups all-purpose flour
1 teaspoon baking soda
1 cup oatmeal

Coffee-Date Filling:

8-ounce package pitted dates, chopped
1 cup sugar
1/2 cup triple-strength coffee
1/2 cup pecans, chopped

Prepare Coffee-Date filling by combining ingredients except pecans in a medium saucepan. Stir over medium heat until dates are very tender and filling is thick and smooth. Stir in pecans. Cool to room temperature. Set aside. Preheat oven to 325 degrees. Generously oil a 12x8-inch baking pan; set aside. Combine melted butter or margarine, brown sugar and coffee in a large bowl. Blend well. Sift together flour and baking soda and combine with oatmeal. Add to butter-sugar mixture. Beat well to blend. Spread half of dough over bottom of prepared pan. Cover with cooled Coffee-Date Filling. Spread remaining dough over filling. Bake for 40 to 45 minutes. Cool to room temperature. Lift edges with spatula. Cut into 1" squares and place on rack to dry slightly. Makes 96 squares.

Where in the Heck is Conway, Arkansas

HALF WAY BETWEEN
PICKLES GAP and TOAD SUCK

Mocha Pecan Logs

1 cup light brown sugar, lightly packed

1/3 cup evaporated milk

2 tablespoons light corn syrup

1 cup semi-sweet chocolate pieces

1 teaspoon instant coffee granules

1 teaspoon vanilla extract

1 cup pecans, chopped

Grease a large cookie sheet and set aside. In a heavy medium saucepan, combine brown sugar, milk and corn syrup. Bring to a boil over medium heat, stirring constantly. Boil and stir 2 minutes. Remove from heat. Add chocolate pieces, coffee and vanilla, stirring until chocolate melts. With a wooden spoon, beat until thick and smooth. Stir in pecans. Spoon onto prepared cookie sheet in 2 equal parts. Shape each half into a 10'' long log. Wrap each log in waxed paper. Refrigerate about 2 hours or until firm. Cut into 20 pieces. Makes 40 pieces.

Chewy Brownie Cookies

2/3 cup Crisco shortening

1-1/2 cups packed light brown sugar

1 tablespoon water

1 teaspoon vanilla extract

2 eggs

1-1/2 cups all purpose flour

1/3 cup cocoa

1/2 teaspoon salt

1/4 teaspoon baking soda

2 cups (12-ounce bag) semi-sweet chocolate chips

Heat oven to 375 degrees. Place length of foil on flat surface. In large bowl, beat shortening, brown sugar, water and vanilla on medium speed of electric mixer until well blended. Add eggs; beat well. Stir together flour, cocoa, salt, and baking soda. Gradually add to sugar mixture, beating on low speed just until blended. Stir in chocolate chips. Drop by rounded tablespoonfuls 2-inches apart onto ungreased cookie sheet. Bake 7 to 9 minutes, or until cookies are set. Cookies will appear soft and moist. Do not overbake. Cool 2 minutes; remove from cookie sheet to foil. Cool completely. Makes about 3 dozen cookies.

Delectable Date Drops

1 cup pitted dates, chopped fine
1/2 cup water
1 egg
1/2 cup brown sugar
1/2 cup butter or margarine
1/4 cup milk
1-1/2 cups all-purpose flour
1/2 teaspoon salt
1/2 teaspoon baking powder
1/4 teaspoon baking soda
1/2 cup nuts, chopped

Combine dates and water and bring to a boil. Simmer five minutes and cool. Set aside 2 tablespoons of date mixture for frosting. Beat in eggs, sugar, butter, and milk. Stir together flour, salt, baking powder and soda. Add to egg mixture. Stir in nuts. Drop from teaspoon onto an ungreased cookie sheet. Bake in 375 degree oven for 10 to 12 minutes. Cool. Frost with date frosting. Beat together:

3 tablespoons softened butter
1-1/2 cups sifted powdered sugar
1/2 teaspoon vanilla
Reserved dates
Enough milk to make spreadable

Makes 3 dozen.

Ruth Hankins

Chocolate Walnut Candy-Cookies

2 packages (6-ounce each) semi-sweet chocolate chips
3 tablespoons soft butter or margarine
3/4 cup sugar
1 egg, unbeaten
1-1/2 teaspoons vanilla
1 tablespoon milk
1/2 cup flour
1/4 teaspoon baking powder
1/2 teaspoon salt
1-1/2 cups walnuts, chopped

Melt one 6-ounce package chocolate over hot, not boiling, water. Stir together butter, sugar, egg and vanilla; beat with spoon just till smooth. Stir in melted chocolate and milk, then flour sifted with baking powder and salt. Stir in nuts and second package chocolate chips. Drop by teaspoonfuls on ungreased cookie sheet. Bake for 10 minutes only at 350 degrees. Cookies will be soft. Cool slightly and remove to rack. Makes 3-1/2 to 4 dozen cookies. Crisp on the outside, chewy inside.

Pete Pleva

Many people are too busy making a living to make life worth living.

62

Old Fashioned Teacakes

1 cup butter, softened
2 cups sugar
3 eggs
2 tablespoons buttermilk
5 cups all-purpose flour
1 teaspoon baking soda
1 teaspoon vanilla extract
Additional sugar

Cream butter; gradually add sugar beating well. Add eggs, one at a time, beating well after each. Add buttermilk and beat well. Combine flour and soda; gradually stir into creamed mixture. Stir in vanilla. Chill dough several hours. Roll dough to 1/4" thickness on a lightly floured surface; cut into rounds with a 3-1/2 " cutter. Place 1" apart on lightly greased cookie sheets; sprinkle with sugar. Bake at 350 degrees for 7 minutes or until edges are very lightly browned. Remove cookies to cool. Makes 4 dozen.

Cyndi Bailey

Chocolate Drop Cookies

1-3/4 cups flour
1/2 cup white sugar
1/2 cup brown sugar
1/2 cup butter
1/2 cup peanut butter
1 egg
1 teaspoon vanilla

2 teaspoons milk
1 teaspoon soda
Unwrapped Hersey's Kisses

Mix all ingredients together except Kisses. Make a small ball - do not mash down. Bake 10 minutes at 375 degrees. Place a chocolate candy kiss in center. Mash down and return to oven for 1 minute.

Robin Clark

Cape Cod Oatmeal Cookies

1 cup butter or shortening, melted
1 cup brown sugar
1/2 cup white sugar
1 egg
1 heaping tablespoon syrup
1 teaspoon soda
1 teaspoon cinnamon
1 teaspoon nutmeg
1-3/4 cups oats
1-1/2 cups flour
1 cup nuts
1 cup raisins
1/4 cup buttermilk

Mix ingredients as written. Put dab, about the size of walnuts, on cookie sheet (approximately 20 per sheet). Bake at 350 degrees until done.

Nanny Young

Treasured Delight

2 cups butter
2 cups white sugar
2 cups brown sugar
4 eggs
5 cups oatmeal
1 teaspoon salt
4 cups flour
2 teaspoons baking powder
2 teaspoons vanilla
24-ounces chocolate chips
8-ounce Hershey's bar, grated
3 cups nuts, chopped

Preheat oven to 375 degrees. Process oatmeal to make "oat flour" in blender or food processor. Cream butter and sugars. Add eggs and vanilla. Mix together with remaining dry ingredients. Add chips, candy and nuts. Roll into balls and place 2" apart on cookie sheet. Bake for 6 to 10 minutes. Recipe can be cut in half. Makes 112 cookies.

"Feeding our ducks will quack you up!"

Hello Dollie Cookies

3/4 cup butter
2-1/4 cups graham cracker crumbs
2 cups chocolate chips
2-1/4 cups coconut
2-1/4 cups walnuts
2 (14-ounce) cans sweetened condensed milk

Pour melted butter onto sheet pan. Apply evenly one layer at a time in order listed above. Pour milk over top (corners and sides too). Bake at 350 degrees about 20 minutes or until golden brown.

Peanut Butter Cookies

1/2 cup butter, softened
1/2 cup peanut butter
1/2 cup sugar
1/2 cup brown sugar
1 egg
1-1/4 cups flour
3/4 teaspoon soda
1/2 teaspoon baking powder
1 teaspoon vanilla
1/4 cup milk

Mix all ingredients in order. Recipe may be doubled and will make 6 dozen. Bake at 375 degrees for 8 to 10 minutes. May substitute oatmeal for part of the flour if desired.

Mrs. Fields' Chocolate Chip Cookies

1 cup butter
1 cup white sugar
1 cup brown sugar
2 eggs
1 teaspoon vanilla
2 cups flour (I like wheat)
2-1/2 cups oatmeal (place oats in blender; make powder, measure)
1/2 teaspoon salt
1 teaspoon baking powder
1 teaspoon baking soda
1-1/2 cups nuts (optional)
12-ounce bag Guittard milk chocolate chips (these are the best - or any other kind)

Cream butter and sugar; add eggs and vanilla. In separate bowl mix all dry ingredients together. Add chips and nuts. Place golf ball size cookies 2" apart on ungreased cookie sheet. Bake at 350 degrees for only 6 minutes.

Peanut Butter Ice Cream

6 eggs
1/2 cup sugar
1/2 cup peanut butter
1-1/2 teaspoons vanilla
1 can Eagle Brand milk
1 pint half and half
1 cup whipping cream
7 plus cups milk

Beat eggs well, add sugar, peanut butter and vanilla. Beat until sugar dissolves. Stir in next three ingredients. Pour into 5-quart ice cream freezer, add milk to freeze line. Freeze.

Ice Cream Crunch

1 quart soft ice cream
1/4 cup brown sugar
1/2 cup nuts, chopped
1 package Dream Whip
1 cup flour
1/4 cup oatmeal
1 stick butter

Mix flour, sugar, oatmeal, nuts and butter in a large bowl. Press mixture on cookie sheet; bake 15 minutes at 350 degrees. Remove from pan; crumble mixture. Place half the crumb mixture in bottom of a baking dish. Spread with ice cream; top with remainder of crumbs and a dip of Dream Whip.

Winter Watermelon

1 pint softened lime sherbet
1/2 gallon softened strawberry ice cream
1 cup chocolate chips

Line Tupperware lettuce crisper with sherbet; chill. Mix ice cream and chips; pour over sherbet; freeze overnight. Remove 20 min. before serving. Unmold; it looks like watermelon.

Marj Hohnbaum

Italian Coffee Ice Cream

1/4 cup almonds
1/4 cup flaked or shredded coconut
1 egg white, room temperature
1/2 cup plus 2 tablespoons granulated sugar, divided
1 cup heavy whipping cream
1 tablespoon instant coffee granules
1 teaspoon vanilla

Place almonds and coconut on cookie sheet. Toast in 300 degree oven 10 minutes or lightly browned; cool slightly. Crush toasted mixture by placing between 2 pieces of waxed paper; press with rolling pin. Beat egg white until stiff; add 2 tablespoons sugar until blended. Whip cream in medium size bowl. Add remaining 1/2 cup sugar, coffee, vanilla and beaten egg white. Beat only to blend. Stir in 1/2 coconut-almond mixture. Spoon tortoni into parfait, sherbet or custard dishes or paper nut cups. Sprinkle remaining coconut-almond mixture on top. Place in freezer for at least 3 hours before serving. Serve directly from freezer. Will keep for several days in freezer. Tortoni is delicious when not completely frozen. Serves 8. Note: If unexpected guests are coming, may be prepared just before eating and placed in freezer while dinner is served. It will be ready to eat for dessert.

Mocha Chip Ice Cream

2 cans sweetened condensed milk
3 egg yolks
1/2 cup triple-strength coffee
1/2 pint whipping cream
2 teaspoons vanilla
1 German chocolate bar, grated
1 cup nuts, chopped
1/2 gallon milk

Mix small amount of condensed milk with egg yolks in blender. Add remaining ingredients except 1/2 gallon milk. Pour into ice cream freezer; fill to line with milk. Freeze as directed. Makes 1 gallon.

Coffee Ice Cream

5 eggs
3 tablespoons flour
3 cups sugar
1 tablespoon vanilla extract
Dash salt
3 cups strong, cold coffee
6 cups half and half

Mix eggs, flour, sugar, vanilla and salt in blender thoroughly. Pour into ice cream freezer; add coffee and half and half. Stir until blended. Churn according to manufacturer's directions for your churn. Makes 4 quarts.

PICKLES, JAMS & JELLIES

How about an Arkansas Products Gift Basket
from Pickles Gap Village? It features
Pickles Gap Jelly, Pickles Gap Sorghum or
Ralph's Bar-B-Q Sauce, Della Arkansas Rice,
Post Muscadine Juice and a Pickles Gap Cook Book.
$34.95
Write for mail order brochure or call 501-327-7708.
(We ship alot of these at Christmas!)

What will it be. . . . pickles or fudge?

Jams and jellies from Pickles Gap Village fill Santa's bag.
Here he's trying to talk Grandma Esther out of one of her
pies!

I'M PICKLED GREEN ABOUT PICKLES GAP VILLAGE!

CONWAY 2 MILES

Pickled Peppers

Green bell peppers

Water

Vinegar

Cloves of garlic

Hot peppers, optional

Boil 2 parts water to 1 part vinegar. Cut peppers in half or quarters. Place peppers and garlic in sterilized jars. Pour liquid over peppers and seal.

Watermelon Rind Pickles

1 large watermelon, (cut into 2-inch squares, remove all red)

3 tablespoons lime

3 quarts water

Syrup:

1-1/2 quarts vinegar

5 pounds sugar

1/2 can allspice

1/2 can stick cinnamon

Cut watermelon rind into 2" squares; remove all red. Soak 3 hours in lime water. Rinse well and put into cold water; bring to a boil. Rinse and repeat two more times. Make syrup. Add watermelon rinds. Bring to a boil and cook 1 hour. Place into hot sterile jars and seal. Makes 6 to 8 quarts.

Sweet Pickle Sticks

Use fresh, firm medium cucumbers. Wash and cut them into sticks. Pour boiling water over them and let stand overnight. Next morning pack solidly into clean jars. Make a solution of:

3-3/4 cups vinegar

3 cups sugar

3 tablespoons salt

4-1/2 teaspoons celery seed

4-1/2 teaspoons turmeric

3/4 teaspoon mustard seed

Boil the solution for 5 minutes; pour boiling hot over cucumbers in jars. Put on caps, screwing tightly. Process in boiling water bath for 5 minutes. Solution fills 6 pint jars or 3 quarts that have been packed with pickles.

Pickled Beets and Eggs

2 cups small beets (canned)
1/4 cup brown sugar
1/2 cup vinegar
1/2 cup cold water
1/2 teaspoon salt
Stick cinnamon
3 cloves
6 hard-boiled eggs
12 teaspoons sugar

Boil all ingredients, except eggs and beets in a saucepan. Add the beets and simmer for several minutes. Cool to just warm and add shelled, boiled eggs. When cool, keep in refrigerator. A Pennsylvania Dutch Recipe.

Bread and Butter Pickles

1 gallon cucumbers
6 larges onions, sliced 1/4-inch thick

Soak overnight in a gallon of water to which 1/2 cup salt has been added. Drain. Mix the following:
1 quart vinegar
2 cups sugar
1 teaspoon each mustard seed, celery seed, and turmeric seed

Boil 15 minutes; pour over cucumbers and onions. Let simmer 20 minutes. Pickles will turn yellow. Put in jars and seal.
Mrs. Estella Spear

Bread and Butter Pickles

4 quarts medium cucumbers (about 24)
2 green peppers, seeded
1/2 cup salt
5 cups cider vinegar
1/2 teaspoon ground cloves
2 teaspoons celery seed
8 small white onions, peeled
5 cups sugar or 4 cups Sugar Twin
1-1/2 teaspoons turmeric
2 tablespoons mustard seed
1 teaspoon red pepper flakes for mild taste

Wash and slice in a large bowl pepper, onions and cucumbers very thin. Add salt and mix well. Cover with ice cubes. Cover bowl and let stand for 3 hours. Drain well. In saucepan, combine sugar, vinegar, turmeric, cloves, mustard seed, celery seed and pepper flakes. Boil for 3 minutes. Add the drained vegetables and bring almost to a boil. This is important, so do not boil! Pack in hot sterilized jars and seal. Makes 6 pints.

"People may doubt what you say, but they will believe what you do."

68

Bread and Butter Pickles

3 quarts sliced cucumbers
1/2 cup salt
1 cup water
1 teaspoon cinnamon
2 tablespoons mustard seed
1/2 tablespoon celery seed
1 piece horseradish, optional
3 onions
3 cups vinegar
3 cups brown sugar
1/2 teaspoon ginger
1 teaspoon turmeric
1 pod hot red pepper

Mix cucumbers, onions and salt. Let stand for 5 hours; drain. Boil vinegar, water, sugar and seasoning for 3 minutes. Add the cucumbers and onions and simmer for 10-20 minutes (do not boil). Pack into hot clean jars and seal at once.

Pickled Eggs

3 to 4 dozen eggs, boiled
3 or 4 bay leaves
4 tablespoons pickling spice
4 tablespoons sugar
Vinegar to fill

Put about 2 cups vinegar in jug or large jar with sugar and spices. Stir to dissolve sugar; put in eggs; fill with vinegar. Set in refrigerator for several days to pickle.

Janis Mack

Pickled Green Beans

1 cup vinegar
1 cup sugar
7 cups water
1 tablespoon salt
1 gallon broken beans

Cook for 35 minutes. Seal in quart or pint jars. To cook: drain off liquid and add enough water to cover. Season with bacon, salt and pepper to taste.

Esther Howard

Marinated Cucumbers

Crisp, different & delicious!

2 medium cucumbers, thinly sliced
1/2 cup sour cream
1 tablespoon lemon juice
1 tablespoon white wine vinegar
1/2 teaspoon salt
1/2 teaspoon sugar
2 tablespoons chives, chopped

Combine ingredients and marinate cucumbers until well chilled.

Betty Morgan

69

Pickled Beets

1 pound can or jar whole beets
1/4 cup vinegar
1/4 cup sugar
1 teaspoon pickling spice, optional

Drain beets, reserving liquid. Mix vinegar and sugar; add to beet liquid and heat until it starts to boil. Add beets and cook for three minutes until heated through and through. Spoon out beets into large jar and finish filling with liquid. Put a lid on it and refrigerate. Will keep a month or longer. (Option: add 1 teaspoon pickling spice while heating beets.)

Esther Howard

Low-Cal Pickled Cranberries

1 pound cranberries, washed
3/4 cup water
8 whole cloves
1/4 cup cider vinegar
1 stick cinnamon
Liquid sweetener to equal
2 cups sugar

Bring water, cloves and cinnamon stick to a boil. Add cranberries; bring to boil again. Cook for 2-3 minutes longer. Remove from heat and add liquid sweetener; store in the refrigerator. Contains 10 calories per 2 tablespoons serving.

Low-Cal Cranberry Relish

1 cup cranberries
Liquid sweetener to taste
1/2 medium orange (remove seeds, but use rind)

Grind cranberries and orange rind together. Let stand several hours. Add sweetener. 1/4 cup may be used with substituting an exchange in your diet.

Low-Cal Pickled Peach Halves

3/4 cup vinegar
1 stick cinnamon, broken
1/2 teaspoon whole cloves - less if you don't like spicy foods

Simmer for 5 minutes. Remove from heat; add:
liquid sweetener to equal
3/4 cup sugar
3/4 cup syrup from dietetic peaches

Pour the spicy vinegar over the dietetic peaches; marinate for several hours or overnight. The liquid my be reused. Two peach halves equal 40 calories.

Low-Cal Curried Broiled Peach Halves

2 dietetic peach havles, cut side up

Sprinkle with curry powder and a few drop of butter flavoring. Broil until hot (10 to 15 minutes). Two peach halves equal 40 calories.

Low-Cal Philadelphia Relish

1 cup cabbage, shredded
1/8 teaspoon mustard seed
1/4 teaspoon salt
Liquid sweetener to equal
2 tablespoons sugar
1 green pepper, chopped
1/2 teaspoon celery seed
2 tablespoons vinegar

Mix and let stand for 1 hour before serving.

Low-Cal Sweet Pickles

12-ounce jar sour pickles
1/2 stick cinnamon
6 whole cloves
Liquid sweetener to equal
1 cup sugar

Pour liquid from pickles into saucepan; add cloves, cinnamon stick and bring to a rolling boil. Take saucepan from burner and add liquid sweetener. Pour over pickles and recap. These are better after being in the refrigerator several days.

Dill Pickles

2 quarts water
1 quart vinegar
1 scant cup salt
5 or 6 pounds cucumbers
Garlic and dill

Bring water, vinegar and salt to boil. Pack cucumbers in jars as tight as possible. Place head of dill and clove of garlic in each quart jar. Pour hot boiling vinegar mixture over cucumbers. Have lids hot. Place in jar and seal. Allow to stay in jars 2 or 3 weeks before opening for better taste.

Sweet Sliced Pickles

16 medium cucumbers
4 cups vinegar
5 tablespoons coarse salt
8 cups sugar
2 tablespoons mixed spice

Cover cucumbers with boiling water; let stand overnight. Repeat 3 times. On the fifth day, drain and slice. Combine sugar, salt, spice and vinegar; bring to a boil and pour over cucumbers. Let stand for 2 days. On the third day, drain liquid into a pan and bring to a boil. Pour over packed cucumbers in hot jars and seal.

"BABE" GHERKIN
DESIGNATED PICKLE
FOR THE
PICKLES GAP VILLAGE
"PICKLES"

Fresh Kosher Style Dill Pickles

Cucumbers

3 cups water

Fresh dill or 1/4 teaspoon dill seed

3 cups cider vinegar

6 tablespoons coarse salt

Fresh garlic or 1/2 tablespoon garlic salt

Wash cucumbers. Soak overnight in 1 tablespoon alum per gallon of water. Make a brine of vinegar, water and salt. Place dill and garlic in bottom of quart jar and fill jars with cucumbers. Add another layer of dill and fill jars to within 1/2" of the top with boiling brine. Seal.

Polish Dills

20-30 (4-inch) cucumbers

Garlic cloves

Powdered alum

Fresh dill

Hot peppers

Brine:

1 cup coarse salt

3 quarts water

Grape leaves

1 tablespoon pickling spice

1 quart cider vinegar

Wash cucumbers. Let stand in ice water overnight. Pack in sterilized jars. To each quart jar, add:

2 heads of dill

1 hot pepper

1 clove garlic

1/8 teaspoon alum

Combine salt, spices, water and vinegar. Heat to a boil. Fill jars; put grape leaves in each jar and seal.

Cold Water Dill Pickles

Brine:

3/4 cup pickling salt

8 cups cold water

2 cups 4 or 8 percent cider vinegar

To each quart, add:

4 large fresh sprigs of dill

1/4 teaspoon cream of tartar

1/4 teaspoon powdered alum or 3 large lumps solid alum

Rinse pickles off. (Important - never soak in water.) Put two sprigs dill in clear jars; add cucumbers, alum, cream of tarter and 2 dill heads on top. Now add cold brine to cover and put lid on tight. Keep at room temperature for six days. Pickles must work in jars. They will not spoil. Store in cool dark place. They are ready to eat in eight weeks. Factory secret: NEVER SOAK CUCUMBERS in water. They fill with water and can't soak up the brine.

72

Five-Day Sweet Pickles

Wash and put into crock container 10 large cucumbers. Cover with boiling water. Add:

5 tablespoons plain salt

Let set in a cool place for three days. On the fourth day, heat:

4 cups vinegar

2 tablespoons mixed pickling spice

8 cups sugar

Heat to a boil; pour over drained cucumbers that have been cut in thick chunks. On the fifth day, heat vinegar mixture. Pack cucumber in sterilized jars. Pour hot mixture over cucumbers; seal. Let set for about two weeks before eating for the best flavor.

Candied Cucumbers

16 pounds cucumbers

1 gallon vinegar

1/2 box alum

10 pounds sugar

1-1/2 boxes pickling spices

Soak in salt brine (strong enough to float an egg) for two weeks. Remove from brine; slice cucumbers 1/2" thick. Cover with alum water; soak overnight. Wash cucumbers; pour vinegar over them. Let stand 4 hours. Drain vinegar and discard. In a large container, alternate cucumbers, sugar and spices, until all are used. Let stand four days. Pack into sterilized jars. These do not have to be sealed.

Aristocrat Pickles

2 cups pickling salt

4 quarts thinly sliced cucumbers

1 tablespoon ground ginger

2 cups water

1 stick cinnamon

1 teaspoon whole cloves

4 quarts water

1 tablespoon powdered alum

2 cups white vinegar

6 cups sugar

1 teaspoon celery seed

1/2 teaspoon whole allspice

Dissolve salt in four quarts of water; add cucumbers; let stand 8 days. Drain well. Add fresh unsalted water to cover; add alum; simmer for 30 minutes. Drain. Add fresh unsalted water to cover; add ginger; simmer again for 30 minutes. Drain well. Mix vinegar, 2 cups water, sugar and spices. Add cucumbers; simmer until pickles are clear. Pack in hot sterilized pint jars; seal. Process 10 minutes in boiling water bath. Makes 6 pints.

Squash Pickles

20-30 medium
yellow squash
2 sweet peppers
5 cups cider vinegar
2 tablespoons mustard seed
1/2 teaspoon cloves
8 large onions
1/2 cup salt
5 cups sugar
1 teaspoon turmeric

Slice squash thin; chop onions and peppers. Mix in salt and let stand for 3 hours. Mix other ingredients and bring to a boil; add squash, onions and pepper. Heat, but do not boil. Pack in jars and seal.

Pepper Relish

1 dozen red bell peppers
Boiling water to cover
3 tablespoons salt
2-1/2 cups sugar
1 dozen green bell peppers
4 large onions, ground
3 cups vinegar

Remove seeds from halved peppers; grind and allow to stand 10 minutes. Drain and cover with boiling water. Let stand 10 minutes; drain. Add sugar, salt, vinegar and onions. Cook 25-30 minutes; place in hot sterile jars; seal. You can add one or two hot peppers.

Zucchini Pickle Relish

Grind and let stand overnight:
4 cups onions
10 cups squash, don't peel
5 tablespoons salt

Cover with cold water. The next day drain off salt water and rinse once in clear water; drain. Add:
2-1/4 cups vinegar
1 tablespoon nutmeg
1 tablespoon dry mustard
1 tablespoon turmeric
1 tablespoon cornstarch
1/2 teaspoon black pepper
1 red bell pepper, chopped
6 cups sugar
2 teaspoons celery seed
1 green bell pepper, chopped

Cook for 30 minutes and seal in hot sterilized jars.

Canned Squash, Okra or Green Tomatoes

1 gallon sliced squash
2-1/2 tablespoons salt
6 tablespoons white vinegar

Dissolve salt, vinegar and enough water to cover sliced squash. Boil 6 minutes, put in jars with vinegar mixture. Seal; put in hot bath 15 minutes. To cook: drain in colander; rinse well with cold water. Roll in flour or cornmeal and deep fry.

Sweet and Sour Dill Pickles

Medium size cucumbers to fill four quart size jars

1 onion, sliced

2 celery stalks, quartered

8 heads fresh dill

4 cups white sugar

2 cups water

1 quart vinegar

1/2 cup canning salt

Wash cucumbers; cut into chunks, enough to fill four quarts. To each jar add: 3 or 4 slices of onion, 2 pieces of celery and 2 heads of dill. Dissolve sugar and salt in vinegar and water; bring to a boil. Place cucumbers in jars, then cover with hot sugar, salt, vinegar and water. Seal at once. For best results, do not use for 30 days. Makes 4 quarts.

Pear Relish

1 peck pears

12 large bell peppers

1 pint prepared mustard

3 cups vinegar

12 large onions

Hot pepper to taste

3 cups sugar

1 tablespoon salt

Grind pears; drain and throw away juice. Grind peppers; drain and throw away juice. Grind onions; save the juice. Mix all ingredients together; add onion juice and cook slowly until tender. Seal in hot jars.

Indian Relish

Prepare and grind:

2 quarts green tomatoes

6 medium onions

1 small head cabbage

12 green peppers

Mix the ingredients and stir in:

1/4 cup salt

Let stand overnight in a cool place. Drain and place in a large kettle and add:

1/2 cup mustard seed

1 cup sugar

1 tablespoon celery seed

1-1/2 cups vinegar

Cook for 5 minutes after it comes to a boil; stir to keep from sticking. Remove from heat and stir in:

1 tablespoon dry mustard

Mix together:

1/2 cup vinegar

3/4 cup chili powder

Add to relish. Mix well and pour into hot jars and seal. Makes 10 pints.

Crisp Cucumber Slices

1/2 cup salt

8 onions, thinly sliced

4 cups sugar

1/2 teaspoon cloves

4-1/2 cups vinegar

4 quarts sliced cucumbers

2 green peppers, cut into strips

1-1/2 teaspoons turmeric

3-1/2 teaspoons mustard seed

Sprinkle salt over the sliced vegetable mix. Put a tray of ice cubes in the center of the vegetables and let stand for 3 hours. Combine sugar, spices and vinegar and heat to boiling. Drain cucumbers; pour hot syrup over them. Heat to scalding, stirring frequently. Pour into sterilized jars; seal and process in boiling water bath for 5 minutes. Makes 5-1/2 pints. Small whole cucumbers may be used if you prefer.

Pickled Mushrooms

1-1/2 pounds fresh mushrooms

1 clove garlic, crushed

3/4 cup salad oil

1/4 cup olive oil

1/2 cup lemon juice

1 cup chopped onion

1 teaspoon salt

1/2 teaspoon pepper

1/2 teaspoon dry mustard

Clean mushrooms; mix with remaining ingredients. Refrigerate in covered container for 24 hours. Put in saucepan; bring to boil; boil 10 minutes; cool. Drain to serve. Will keep for weeks in the refrigerator. Makes 3 to 4 dozen.

Peach Pickles

8 pounds peeled peaches

3 pounds sugar

4 sticks cinnamon

2 tablespoons whole cloves, crushed

1 tablespoon fresh ginger

1 quart vinegar

Wash and peel peaches. Treat to prevent darkening. Dissolve sugar in vinegar in large saucepan and heat. Boil 5 minutes and skim. Add spices tied in a cheesecloth bag. Drop drained peaches into boiling syrup and cook until they can be pierced with a fork, but not soft. Remove from heat and allow peaches to set in pickling liquid overnight to plump. Bring to a boil. Pack peaches into hot jars, leaving 1/4" head space. Pour hot liquid over peaches, 1/4" head space. Remove air bubbles. Adjust caps. Process 20 minutes in boiling water bath. Makes about three quarts.

Tomato Relish

20 cups ripe tomatoes, peeled and cored

8 onions, chopped

8 bell peppers, chopped

6 tablespoons salt

1/2 cup hot peppers, chopped

3 cups sugar

1/2 box pickling spice

3 cups vinegar

Chop, mix and cook slowly after reaching boiling point. Cook at least 2 hours. Stir often. Pour in jars and seal.

Okra Pickles

3-1/2 pounds small okra pods

4 cloves garlic

2 small hot peppers, cut in half

3 cups water

3 cups vinegar

1/3 cup canning salt

2 teaspoons dill seed

Pack okra firmly into hot jars, leaving 1/4" head space. Put a garlic clove and half a pepper in each jar. Combine water, vinegar, salt and dill seed; bring to boil. Pour hot liquid over okra leaving a 1/4" head space. Remove air bubbles. Adjust caps. Process 15 minutes in boiling water bath. Makes four pints.

Marinated Carrots

1 or 2 pounds carrots

1 can tomato soup

1/2 cup sugar

1/2 cup oil

1/2 cup vinegar

1 purple onion, sliced

1 green pepper, chopped

Slice carrots like pennies, 1/2" wide. Boil sliced carrots until tender. Boil next 4 ingredients; pour over sliced carrots. Add and arrange onion and chopped pepper in large serving bowl.

Green Tomato Pickles

6 quarts green tomatoes, quartered

1 cup red bell peppers, sliced

3/4 cup pickling salt

2 quarts onions, chopped

1 cup jalapeno peppers, chopped

Sprinkle salt over vegetables and let set overnight; drain well. Bring to boil:

6 cups sugar

1 teaspoon mustard seed

1/2 gallon white vinegar

Add vegetables to boiling liquid; cook until vegetables change color. Put into jars and seal.

Refrigerator Bread & Butter Pickles

2 cups cucumbers, sliced
1 cup onions, chopped
1 cup sugar
1/2 cup vinegar
1 teaspoon salt
1/2 teaspoon mustard seed
1/2 teaspoon turmeric

Microwave 10 minutes, stir every 3 minutes.

Old Fashioned Corn Relish

1/4 cup sugar
1/2 cup vinegar
1/2 teaspoon salt
1/4 teaspoon hot sauce
1/2 teaspoon celery seed
1/4 teaspoon mustard seed
12-ounce can whole kernel corn
2 tablespoons green pepper, chopped
2 tablespoons pimento, chopped
1 tablespoon minced onion

Combine sugar, salt, vinegar, hot sauce and seeds. Boil 2 minutes, then combine with other ingredients.

Pepper Relish

4 cups onions
4 cups cabbage
4 cups green pepper (bell & hot)
4 cups green tomatoes
6 cups sugar
1 tablespoon white mustard seed
1-1/2 teaspoons turmeric
4 cups apple cider vinegar
2 cups water
1/2 cup salt

Make measurements after grinding vegetables. Sprinkle 1/2 cup salt over ground vegetables. Let set overnight. Rinse and drain. Mix sugar, spices, vinegar and water. Bring to a boil. Add ground mixture to liquid. Pour into jars and seal. May be processed in pressure cooker 5 pounds for 5 minutes. Use a variety of peppers; bell, jalapeno, banana, etc.

Squash Relish

8 cups squash
3 large onions
3 cucumbers
6 green tomatoes
2 bell peppers, red

Chop or shred vegetables. Sprinkle 2 tablespoons red pepper flakes and 3 teaspoons canning salt. Put ice on top; cover; refrigerate overnight. Drain and rinse. Add 3 to 3-1/2 cups sugar, 2-1/2 cups cider vinegar, 1/2 teaspoon celery seed, 2 teaspoons turmeric and 2 teaspoons ground mustard. Bring to boil and simmer 30 minutes. Seal jars.

Green Tomato Pickles

2 quarts green tomatoes
2 large green peppers
2 or 3 hot peppers
3 tablespoons salt
2 cups vinegar
2 cups white sugar
2/3 cup brown sugar
1 teaspoon turmeric
3 tablespoons mustard seed
1/2 teaspoon celery seed
3 cups onion, sliced or chopped

Chunk green tomatoes; chop peppers. Sprinkle salt over above and let stand 10-12 hours. Drain, put mustard seed and celery seed in bag and boil 5 minutes in mixture of vinegar, sugars and turmeric. Add the onions; cook for 5 minutes. Add green tomatoes and peppers; simmer for 5 minutes. Put in jars; cover with syrup and seal.

Swiss Pickles

12 medium peppers
6-1/2 cups sugar
1 bottle fruit pectin
1-1/2 cups vinegar

Green and red sweet peppers may be used in any proportion. Discard seeds. Put peppers through food chopper twice using finest knife. Measure peppers. Use enough juice from peppers to make cups level. Add sugar and vinegar. Mix thoroughly. Heat rapidly to a full rolling boil; stir constantly before and while boiling. Boil hard 2 minutes. Remove from heat; stir in pectin. Stir and skim alternately for just 8 minutes to cool slightly to prevent floating.

Virginia Chunk Sweet Pickles

75 cucumbers, 4-5" long, or 2 gallons small ones
Canning salt

Make brine (2 cups salt to 1 gallon water); boil; pour over cucumbers. Weight down to keep submerged. Let stand 1 week; skim daily. Drain; cut into chunks. Next 3 mornings, make boiling solution of 1 gallon water and 1 tablespoon alum. Pour over drained pickles. Fourth Morning: drain-discard alum water. Heat 6 cups vinegar, 5 cups sugar, 1/3 cup pickling spice and 1 tablespoon celery seed to boiling; pour over pickles. Fifth Morning: drain in pan; add 2 cups sugar, boil; pour over pickles. Sixth Morning: drain in pan; add 1 cup sugar; heat; pack pickles in sterilized jars. Fill to within 1/2" of top of jar with boiling liquid. Seal at once.

Tips to New Cooks About Jelly Making

When in doubt about jelly and jam making, go buy a box of Sure-Jell and you will make perfect jelly or jam everytime! Only make small amounts of jelly or jams at a time. Store juice and fruits in freezer and make as you need it. Flavor stays fresh tasting for a long time.

Canning Fruit Without Sugar

Any fruit, such as peaches, pears, etc. may be canned at home by following the usual directions for canning, except that you omit the sugar. You may can fruit in its own juice by adding just enough water to fill the jar. You will find directions in most any cookbook telling you how much time should be used to steam the different fruits. The fruit will keep well when the can is sealed properly.

Low-Cal Grape Jelly

1 envelope plain gelatin
1 grain grape juice, unsweetened
4 teaspoons lemon juice
1/2 cup cold water
3 tablespoons grated lemon rind
Pinch of salt

Place gelatin in 1/2 cup cold water; add saccharin. Allow gelatin to soften. Bring 1 cup grape juice to boil; add to gelatin. Stir until dissolved. Add other cup of grape juice, lemon juice, rind, and salt. Pour into jelly glasses. When cold, cover with lid; keep refrigerated. It must be treated like any gelatin dessert. It must be refrigerated when not being eaten. Contains 16 calories per serving.

Low-Cal Strawberry Jelly

2 teaspoons unflavored gelatin
1 cup crushed strawberries
Artificial sweetener to equal
4 teaspoons sugar
3/4 cup water
1/2 teaspoon vanilla extract

Dissolve gelatin in hot water in saucepan. Add remaining ingredients; pour into small dish. Chill. Makes 4 servings.

Jalapeno Jelly

1 pound green peppers
1/4 pound jalapeno
peppers
5-1/2 cups sugar
1-1/4 cups white vinegar
(5 percent acidity)
1/3 cup fresh lemon juice
2 (3-ounce) packages liquid
fruit pectin

Wash peppers, pat dry. Trim, seed and remove veins; cut into quarters; set aside. Position steel blade in food processor bowl. Add peppers; process about 1-1/2 minutes or until smooth (pulp will be visible). Combine peppers, sugar and vinegar in Dutch oven. Bring to boil. Boil 5 minutes, stirring constantly. Stir in lemon juice; return to boil. Add pectin; return to boil. Boil 1 minute, stirring constantly. Remove from heat; skim off foam with metal spoon. Quickly pour jelly into hot, sterilized jars, filling to 1/4" from top; wipe jar rims. Cover at once with metal lids and screw on bands. Process in boiling water bath for 5 minutes or let cool 12 hours; store in refrigerator. Serve over cream cheese with fresh fruit and crackers. Makes 8-1/2 pints. Note: Always wear rubber gloves when working with hot peppers such as jalapenos! *Becky Poe*

Watermelon Rind Preserves

Select melons with thick rinds; peel off outside peel, leaving white and a small portion of the ripe. Cut into small dices. Soak in mild salt water overnight (1/2 cup salt to 1 gallon water). Remove from salt water; cook in clear water for 30 minutes or until tender; drain well. For 4-pounds (11 cups) of melon rind, make a syrup of:

9 cups sugar
4 lemon slices
8 cups water
Add:
4 sticks cinnamon
4 teaspoons whole cloves

Tie spices in cheesecloth bag. Boil syrup and spices 5 minutes before adding rinds. Add rinds; cook until transparent and clear. If desired, a few drops of food coloring, red or green to tint preserves, may be added 4 or 5 minutes before removing from heat. Remove spice bag; pour into sterilized jars. Seal. NOTE: This recipe came from an old Kerr Canning book.

*"There is no better exercise
for the heart than
reaching down and
lifting someone up."*

Quick Peach Preserves

9 cups firm peaches, peeled, pitted and sliced

3/4 cup water

6 cups sugar

Boil peaches in water till tender; stir often. Strain; reserve. Add sugar to juices; boil till mixture spins thread (233 degrees). Return peaches to pan; cook rapidly 15 minutes. Pour into sterilized jars; seal. Makes about 2 pints.

Pear Honey

6 pears

1 orange

2 apples

8 cups sugar

Grind pears, apples and orange; add sugar. Cook for 20 minutes, stir often. Add grated orange rind; cook until thick. Pour into sterilized jars. This is so good!

Freezer Strawberry Jam

3 cups mashed berries

3/4 cup water

5 cups sugar

1 box Sure-Jell

Combine berries and sugar; let set for about 10 minutes. Stir several times to dissolve sugar. Combine water and Sure-Jell in saucepan; bring to full rolling boil for 1 minute. Pour into berries; stir until foam disappears. Ladle into jars. Let set at room temperature until jam jells. Store in freezer.

Muscadine Jelly

1 quart muscadine juice

3 cups sugar

Wash and pick over about 3 quarts muscadines. Crush and for each gallon of fruit, add 1 cup of water. Simmer 15 minutes. Strain through colander without pressing, then strain through jelly bag. Let chill 2 or 3 hours. Heat juice to boiling. Add sugar; boil rapidly until sugar dissolves. Test by letting syrup run off side of spoon when held above pot. When steady stream of syrup is broken, it has reached jelly stage. Pour into jelly glasses; seal. Makes 6-8.

Grape Arbor Jelly

1-1/2 pounds Arkansas grapes

1-1/2 pounds sugar

Put grapes in heavy saucepan; add sugar. Bring to boil; simmer 25 minutes. Strain through sieve; pour into sterilized jars; seal. Makes 2-1/2 pints.

"Very few people are big enough to become small enough for God to use."

82

PIES, PUDDINGS & COBBLERS

If you don't feel like baking, just stop by the Pickle Barrel Restaurant for lunch and sample some of our homemade pies and cobblers. If you want a real treat, try a piece of Grandma Esther's Coconut or Chocolate pie!
(Look for pie recipes in this section.)

Grandma Esther
with her famous pies
at the Pickle Barrel
Restaurant.

Grandma Esther's chocolate and coconut pies.

Low-Fat Basic Graham Cracker Crust

1-1/2 cups crushed graham crackers (eight full-sized graham crackers)

2 tablespoons sugar

1-1/2 tablespoons liquid Butter Buds

Crush the graham crackers by placing squares on a piece of waxed paper and rolling over them with a rolling pin. Place all the ingredients and mix with a fork until moistened. Press into a pie pan that has been sprayed with a non-fat cooking spray. Makes one 8-9 inch crust.

Low-Fat Strawberry Cream Cheese Pie

Crust:

2 large flour tortillas

1/2 teaspoon Molly McButter Buttermist or other butter-flavored nonstick cooking spray

Preheat oven to 350 degrees. Place 1 tortilla in deep 9-1/2" pie plate sprayed with nonstick cooking spray. Spray tortilla lightly with butter spray and sprinkle with Molly McButter. Place second tortilla on top and spray lightly with butter spray. Spray outside bottom of another empty pie plate and set it down inside and on top of tortilllas for baking. Bake for 13 minutes. Remove and cool; remove extra pie plate. Cool thoroughly before adding filling.

Filling:

1 envelope Knox unflavored gelatin

1/2 cup hot water

16-ounce package frozen strawberries with sugar

12-ounce carton Kraft fat-free cream cheese

1/3 cup sugar

Stir gelatin into hot water until dissolved. Combine with remaining ingredients in food processor and mix. Pour into prepared crust.

Topping:

1/2 envelope Knox unflavored gelatin

1/2 cup hot water

1-1/2 cups fat-free sour cream

1/3 cup sugar

1/2 teaspoon vanilla extract

Stir gelatin into hot water until dissolved. Combine with remaining ingredients and mix with electric mixer. Pour gently over filling. Chill several hours or overnight. Recipe makes 10 servings.

"A good test of a person's character is his behavior when he is wrong."

Low-Fat Fake Pecan Pie

Crust:
2 large flour tortillas

Buttermist or other butter-flavored nonstick cooking spray

1/2 teaspoon Molly McButter

Place 1 tortilla in 9" pie plate spray with nonstick cooking spray. Spray tortilla and sprinkle with Molly McButter. Repeat with second tortilla. Using another 9" pie plate, spray outside bottom and place on top of tortillas. This helps press and form pie crust. Bake crust with pie plate on top at 350 degrees for 7 minutes. Cool slightly while preparing filling.

Filling:
3/4 cup Healthy Choice liquid egg product

1/2 cup light corn syrup

1 cup brown sugar

1 teaspoon flour

1 tablespoon Molly McButter

1 teaspoon vanilla extract

1/3 cup Grape Nuts cereal

In large bowl, combine all ingredients except Grape Nuts and mix with electric mixer. Pour into partially baked crust. Sprinkle Grape Nuts over top of filling and bake at 350 degrees for 35 minutes. DO NOT cook over 35 minutes or it might spill over sides while baking. Also, do not worry about how it looks while cooking because it will puff up high but will go back down as soon as it cools. Makes 8 servings.

Low-Fat Blackberry Cobbler

Filling:
4 cups frozen blackberries, thawed

3/4 cup sugar

1 teaspoon lemon juice

1 teaspoon Molly McButter

Crust:
1-1/2 cups Pioneer No Fat Bisquit Mix*

1-1/4 cups evaporated skim milk

1/8 cup sugar

Combine filling ingredients. Stir gently until sugar starts to dissolve and set aside. Combine biscuit mix and milk; stir until well blended. Mixture will be like thin batter. Add sugar and mix. Pour half the batter into a 9x12" baking dish sprayed with nonstick cooking spray. Spoon berry mixture evenly over top. Pour remaining batter evenly over berries. Sprinkle spoonful of granulated sugar over top. Bake at 350 degrees for 30 minutes. Serve hot or cold. Makes 8 servings. *If you can't find Pioneer No Fat Bisquit Mix in your area, use a light biscuit mix.

Low-Fat Chocolate Chip Pie

Crust:

1/2 cup Grape Nuts cereal

2-1/2 tablespoons sugar

1/2 teaspoon Molly McButter

Filling:

1 cup Healthy Choice liquid egg product

1-1/3 cups sugar

1/3 cup flour

1-1/2 tablespoons Molly McButter

1 teaspoon vanilla extract

1/4 teaspoon almond extract

1/3 cup fat-free sour cream

1/3 cup regular-size semi-sweet chocolate chips (reserve)

1/3 cup miniature semi-sweet chocolate chips (reserve)

Sprinkle Grape Nuts evenly over bottom of 9" pie plate sprayed with nonstick cooking spray. Sprinkle evenly with 2-1/2 tablespoons sugar and 1/2 teaspoon Molly McButter; set aside. In medium bowl, using mixer, combine egg product, sugar, flour, Molly McButter, vanilla and almond extracts and sour cream. Cream until smooth. Gently pour slowly over Grape Nuts, trying not to disturb crust. Using the 1/3 cup regular-size chocolate chips, take a few at a time and drop each chip on top of filling, then fill in various places until all chips are used. These will gradually sink into filling. Sprinkle miniature chips on top for garnish. Bake at 325 degrees for 50 minutes. Serves 8.

Low-Fat Apple and Raisin Bread Pudding

4 cups french bread, cubed

1-1/2 cups diced apples (green or red delicious, or a mixture)

1/2 cup raisins

1-1/2 cups skim milk

3 Egg Beaters

3/4 cup sugar

2 tablespoons liquid Butter Buds

1 teaspoon vanilla extract

1/2 teaspoon cinnamon

1/4 teaspoon ground nutmeg

In a 2-quart casserole that has been sprayed with a non-fat cooking spray, combine bread cubes, apples and raisins; set aside. Combine milk, Egg Beaters, sugar, liquid Butter Buds, vanilla, cinnamon, and nutmeg; pour over bread mixture. Bake at 350 degrees for 45-50 minutes or until knife inserted in center comes out clean. Serve warm with Dream Whip or non-fat frozen yogurt on top if desired. Serves 8.

Low-Fat Cherry Crunch

1/3 cup light brown sugar

1/4 cup liquid Butter Buds

1 teaspoon cinnamon

1/2 teaspoon nutmeg

2 cups cornflakes cereal

1/2 teaspoon almond extract

1 can (21-ounces) cherry pie filling

1 quart non-fat frozen vanilla yogurt

In a medium bowl, combine sugar, liquid Butter Buds, cinnamon, and nutmeg. Blend until it resembles coarse crumbs. Crush cornflakes slightly. With a fork, mix into sugar mixture. Combine almond extract and cherry pie filling. Turn into a shallow 1-quart baking dish sprayed with a non-fat cooking spray. Top with cornflake mixture, spread evenly. Bake at 375 degrees for 20 minutes, or until top is golden and cherry filling is bubbling. Cool 20-30 minutes. Serve warm, top each piece with frozen yogurt. Serves 6.

Low-Fat Strawberry and Banana Pie

Pastry Pie Crust:

1 cup all-purpose flour

3/4 teaspoon lite salt

1/3 cup light corn syrup

2 tablespoons skim milk

Spray a 9" pie pan with non-fat cooking spray. Mix all the above ingredients until moistened. Form into a ball and roll out on a floured surface to fit pie pan. Don't overwork the dough. Prick bottom of crust; bake at 475 degrees for 10 minutes or until golden brown.

Filling:

1 pint fresh strawberries

3/4 cup water

1/2 cup sugar

2-1/2 tablespoons cornstarch

1 large banana or 2 small ones

Red food coloring

Topping:

1 envelope Dream Whip Mix

1/2 cup cold skim milk

1 teaspoon vanilla

Wash, hull and slice strawberries in half. Place in a saucepan with water and 1/2 teaspoon food coloring; bring to boil. When it reaches a full boil, add sugar and cornstarch that has been mixed together. Stir until thickened and clear. Remove from heat; refrigerate. When cooled, slice banana and layer in bottom of baked cooled crust. Pour strawberry filling over bananas; return to refrigerator until time to serve. Top with one package of prepared Dream Whip. Makes one 9" pie. Serves 6 to 8.

Thinking of you... puts a joyful song in my heart!

Joyce's Pie Crust

5 cups flour

2 cups shortening

2 teaspoons salt

1/2 cup cold water

2 eggs beaten

2 tablespoons vinegar

Sift flour and salt; cut in shortening with flour until it's like coarse cornmeal. Beat eggs; mix with water and vinegar. Combine with flour; toss with a fork to mix lightly. Shape into balls. Freeze unused portion.

Joyce Reynolds

Joyce Reynolds, a dear friend and employee at Mack Realty, has gone to be with the Lord. She left behind a lot of good recipes and sweet memories to be shared with her friends and family. We miss her!
Janis Mack

Chocolate Pie

1 cup sugar

1/2 cup Pet milk

1 cup milk

1/8 teaspoon salt

2-ounces Hershey's all natural semi-sweet chocolate

3 tablespoons flour

1/4 cup whipping cream

3 egg yolks

1 teaspoon vanilla

9-inch baked pie shell

Mix sugar and flour; add pet milk; add egg yolks. Mix 1 minute. Add whipping cream and milk. Add chocolate squares. Put in microwave for 7 to 8 minutes. Add vanilla and salt. Pour into baked pie shell. Beat 3 egg whites until stiff; add 1/4 teaspoon cream of tartar. Beat for 1 minute; add 1/3 cup sugar. Beat for 1 minute. Spread on pie; bake in hot oven until brown.   **Esther Howard**

Cheese Cake

36 graham crackers

1/4-pound butter

3-ounce package lemon jello

1 cup boiling water

8-ounce package cream cheese

1 cup sugar

1 teaspoon vanilla

1 large can Milnot milk (chilled)

Crush graham crackers. Mix with butter; press into bottom of oblong cake pan to form crust. Mix jello with water; let cool until slightly thickened. Whip milk until stiff; mix with jello. Add cream cheese mixture. Pour into crust. Top with additional graham cracker crumbs. Refrigerate at least 12 hours before serving. Makes a large cake.

Anna Allison

Easy Enough Cheese Cake

3.5-ounce package lemon instant pudding

1 cup milk

8-ounce cream cheese

Cream milk and cream cheese with electric mixer. Add pudding mix; mix well. Pour into graham cracker crust and top with your favorite cherry or blueberry pie filling, Cool Whip or whatever!

Maxine Brinsfield

Sugarless Cheese Cake

2 (8-ounce) packages cream cheese, softened

3 large eggs, room temperature

1/2 cup honey

1 teaspoon vanilla (variation- almond extract)

Topping:

1 pint sour cream

1/8 cup honey

1 teaspoon vanilla (variation- almond extract)

Mix egg yolks, cream cheese, honey and vanilla until creamy and smooth. Whip egg whites until stiff; fold into cheese mixture. Do not blend. Fold lightly. Pour into chilled crust. Bake at 350 degrees for about 40 minutes or until pie does not shake like jello in center. It will be browned on top. Remove and cool for 10 minutes; add topping; bake at 400 degrees for 3 to 5 minutes. Remove; cool. Chill about 8 hours before serving. Fits a 10 or 12" spring form pan. Serves about 10. Serve with fresh fruit in season.

Easy (No Bake) Cheese Cake

8-ounce package cream cheese

1 cup powdered sugar

2 cups Cool Whip

1 teaspoon lemon juice

Graham cracher crust

Cherry or blueberry pie filling

Cream together cream cheese and sugar. Fold in Cool Whip; add lemon juice. Blend together with spoon. Pour into graham cracker crust and garnish with cherry or blueberry pie filling on top.   *Janis Mack*

This is a quick and easy pie we make at the Pickle Barrel Restaurant at Pickles Gap Village.!

88

Cheese Cake

1 small package lemon jello
3 lemons
8-ounces cream cheese
1 large can Carnation milk
1 cup boiling water
1 cup sugar
4 drops yellow food color, optional

Crust:

2-1/2 cups graham cracker crumbs
1 stick oleo
1/2 cup sugar

Dissolve jello in boiling water; set in refrigerator. Cream lemon juice (from 3 lemons), sugar and cream cheese until smooth. When jello mix becomes as thick as egg whites unbeaten, add to cream cheese mixture. Chill milk and whip until stiff. Fold in cheese mixture; add yellow color to make it pretty. Pour into cooled crust and top with a few graham cracker crumbs.   *Odessa Davis*

Paradise Pie

3 eggs whites
1 cup sugar
1 teaspoon vanilla
20 soda crackers
1 cup pecans or walnuts, chopped
1 cup whipping cream or Cool Whip

1 small can crushed pineapple, drained
1/2 cup coconut

Beat egg whites, add sugar, slowly and vanilla. Stir in crushed crackers; add nuts. Pour in pie pan. Bake 20 minutes at 325 degrees; cool 1 hour. Mix Cool Whip, pineapple, coconut and spread on top of cooled pie. Chill or freeze until firm.

Jean Young

Sugar Free Strawberry Pie

1 small package sugar-free Vanilla Pudding (cooked variety)
1 small sugar-free strawberry jello
2 cups water
1 teaspoon vanilla flavoring
3 packages artificial sweetener (individual size)
2 cups sliced fresh strawberries
1/8" graham cracker crust

Combine pudding mix, jello, water and vanilla. Cook and stir until thickened. Set aside to cool. Prepare strawberries and sprinkle with sweetener. When pudding mixture has cooled, fold in the strawberry mixture; pour into crust. Refrigerate for an hour or over night before serving. Top with Cool Whip.

Zoe Mack

Butterscotch Pie

1 cup sugar

1/2 cup all-purpose flour

1/2 cup melted butter

2 eggs, slightly beaten

6-ounce package butterscotch chips

1 cup pecans, chopped

1 teaspoon vanilla

9'' unbaked pie shell

Mix sugar and flour together. Add butter; blend well. Stir in chips, nuts and vanilla. Pour into pie shell. Bake in a 325 degree oven for 60 minutes or until golden brown. Pie will wiggle when done; it sets as it cools. Serves 8.

Esther Howard

Chocolate Chip Pie

2 eggs

1 stick butter, melted

1/2 cup all-purpose flour

1 cup granulated sugar

1 teaspoon vanilla

6-ounces chocolate chips

1 cup walnuts

1/4 cup bourbon, optional

Mix all ingredients. Place in unbaked pie shell. Bake at 350 degrees for 40-45 minutes. Do not overcook.

Chess Pie

3/4 stick margarine

2-1/2 cups sugar

6 eggs

2 tablespoons vinegar

2 teaspoons meal

1 tablespoon vanilla

Cream margarine and sugar. Add eggs, vinegar, meal, and vanilla. Pour into unbaked pie shell and bake 300 degrees about 35 minutes until done. Another version: add 1/2 cup coconut or 1 teaspoon lemon flavoring before baking.

Janis Mack

Chess Pie

1 cup butter

3 cups sugar

6 eggs

2 tablespoons vinegar

2 teaspoons meal

1 tablespoon vanilla

Cream butter and sugar. Add eggs until well blended. Add vanilla, vinegar and meal. Pour in unbaked pie shell. Bake at 300 degrees for 35 minutes. 1/2 cup coconut may be added if desired or 1 teaspoon lemon flavoring. Makes two pies.

Jean Sawrie

Peanut Butter Pie

Filling:

2 cups milk

1 cup sugar

2 egg yolks

4 tablespoons cornstarch

1 teaspoon vanilla

Crust:

1 stick margarine, melted

1 cup flour

2 tablespoons powdered sugar

Peanut Butter Mixture:

3 tablespoons peanut butter

4-5 tablespoons powdered sugar

Cook filling ingredients together until thick. Mix crust ingredients together. Pat crust mixture out into a pie plate; bake 15 to 20 minutes at 350 degrees or until done. While crust is hot, sprinkle peanut butter mixture over crust, add hot pie filling then prepare meringue and cover pie with meringue. Sprinkle a little of the peanut buttler mixture over the top of the meringue before you brown it.

Louise Vann

Pecan Pie

3 tablespoons butter or margarine

2/3 cup light brown sugar

Pinch of salt

3/4 cup light corn syrup

1/2 cup canned milk

3 eggs

3/4 teaspoon vanilla

Blend mixture and add 1 cup chopped pecans or whole pecans; enough to cover the top of pie. Bake pie for 10 minutes at 450 degrees, then reduce heat to 350 degrees and bake until custard sets about 30 minutes. Serve plain or add whipped topping.   *Zoe Mack*

Mildred's Pecan Pie

1/2 cup butter

1 cup sugar

3 eggs, beaten

3/4 cup corn syrup

1/4 teaspoon salt

1 teaspoon vanilla

1-1/2 cups pecans

1 tablespoon brown sugar

Mix all ingredients together. Bake at 375 degrees for 40-45 minutes or until done in unbaked pie shell.

Helen Belote

Raisin Pie

3 eggs, separated
3 tablespoons butter
1-1/2 cups sugar
1 tablespoon vinegar or lemon juice
2 cups raisins, plumped (soak in hot water for a few minutes)
1 teaspoon vanilla

Cream butter, sugar then add add beaten egg yolks, vinegar or lemon juice, raisins and vanilla. Fold in beaten egg whites. Bake at 325 degrees in an unbaked pie shell until a knife inserted in pie comes out clean.

Diane Hensley

Texas Pie

4 eggs
1-1/2 cups sugar
1/4 cup butter
1 can crushed pineapple
1 cup coconut
1 teaspoon vanilla
10" unbaked pie shell

Mix and bake.

Bernice Burgess

Kentucky Derby Pie

9" pie shell, unbaked
2 eggs, slightly beaten
1 cup sugar
1/2 cup flour
6-ounce package chocolate chips
1/2 cup oleo, melted
1 cup pecans, chopped
1 teaspoon vanilla
2/3 quart vanilla ice cream

Beat eggs slightly; add sugar, flour, melted butter. Stir until blended. Add chips, nuts and vanilla. Pour into pie shell. Bake at 350 degrees for 45 minutes. Serve hot, with ice cream on top.

Cyndi Bailey

Sawdust Pie

7 egg whites, unbeaten
1-1/2 cups granulated sugar
1-1/2 cups graham cracker crumbs
1-1/2 cups pecans
1-1/2 cups coconut
9" unbaked pie shell

Mix all ingredients together and stir. Pour into unbaked pie shell. Bake at 325 degrees until glossy and set, about 25-30 minutes. Do Not Overbake! Serve warm with sliced bananas and whipped cream. Serves 8.

Super Banana Pudding

Mix 2 small boxes instant vanilla pudding with 4 cups cold milk. Add: 1 can Eagle Brand milk and 12-ounce carton Cool Whip. Slice 4 ripe, but firm bananas. Layer vanilla wafers, bananas and pudding mixture. Refrigerate until serving time.

Becky Poe

Sensational Double Layer Pumpkin Pie

4-ounces cream cheese, softened

1 tablespoon milk or half & half

1 tablespoon sugar

1-1/2 cups thawed Cool Whip

1 graham cracker pie crust

1 cup cold milk or half & half

2 packages vanilla instant pudding and pie filling (4-serving size)

16-ounce can pumpkin

1 teaspoon cinnamon

1/2 teaspoon ginger

1/4 teaspoon cloves

Beat cream cheese, 1 tablespoon milk and sugar in large bowl with wire whisk until smooth. Gently stir in whipped topping. Spread on bottom of crust. Pour 1 cup milk into bowl. Add pudding mix. Beat with whisk 1 to 2 minutes. (Mixture will be thick.) Stir in pumpkin and spices with whisk; mix well. Spread over cream cheese layer. Refrigerate 4 hours or until set. Garnish as desired. Store leftover pie in refrigerator. Makes 8 servings.

Helpful Hint: Soften cream cheese in microwave on HIGH 15 to 20 seconds.

Esther's Chocolate Pie

1 cup sugar

1/4 cup plain flour

3 egg yolks

2 tablespoons cocoa

2 cups whole milk

2 tablespoons milk chocolate chips

1 teaspoon vanilla extract

1 baked pie shell

Mix sugar, flour and cocoa well. Add 1/2 cup milk; blend. Add 3 well beaten egg yolks to mixture; mix then add remaining milk. Blend well then stir in chips. Put bowl in microwave and microwave for 4 minutes. Stir thoroughly; let cook another 2 minutes, stir; then microwave another 2 minutes; remove from microwave; stir in 1 teaspoon of vanilla extract. Pour into baked pie shell. Top with meringue and brown at 350 degrees or top with whipped topping when pie is cooled.   *Esther Howard*

Esther's Meringue for Cream Pies

3 large egg whites

1/4 teaspoon cream of tartar

1/3 cup sugar

In a bowl, beat 3 large egg whites and 1/4 teaspoon cream of tartar until stiff. Gradually add the sugar to egg whites, beating for 1 minute. Spread on pie. Brown in 350 degree oven.
          Esther Howard

93

Butterscotch Pecan Pie

9" unbaked pie shell
1 cup sugar
1 cup light corn syrup
1/2 stick butter
1/4 cup real maple syrup
4 eggs beaten
1-1/2 cups butterscotch morsels
2 cups pecan halves, as desired
Ice cream or whipped cream, optional

In saucepan, heat sugar, corn syrup, maple syrup and butter just until butter melts. Blend. Remove from heat; cool to room temperature, stir in eggs. Line bottom pie shell with butterscotch morsels; pour in filling. Arrange pecan halves on top; bake at 325 degrees for 55 minutes. Cool pie; serve cold or at room temperature. Top with ice cream or whipped cream. Makes 10 servings.

Maxine Whayne

Buttermilk Pie

3 eggs
3/4 cup sugar
1 cup buttermilk
1 teaspoon cornmeal
1 teaspoon vanilla
1 teaspoon nutmeg
9" pie shell

Beat eggs, sugar and buttermilk. Add remaining ingredients. Mix well; pour into pie crust.

Bake at 350 degrees for 30 minutes.

Custard Pie

4 eggs
1/4 cup sugar
1/4 teaspoon salt
2 cups milk
1 cup cream
Dash of nutmeg

Line 9" pie pan with pastry. Brush the inside with white of egg. Chill. Beat eggs slightly with fork; add sugar and salt; stir until blended. Add milk and cream; blend well. Gently pour custard into pan. Sprinkle nutmeg on top. Bake at 450 degrees for 10 minutes; reduce heat to 300 degrees for 50 minutes.

Chocolate Silk Pie

3/4 cup butter, softened
3/4 cup sugar
3 eggs
1 teaspoon vanilla
3 squares unsweetened chocolate, melted and cooled
1/2 pint whipping cream
2 tablespoons sugar

Cream butter and sugar. Add eggs, one at a time. Beat well; add vanilla and chocolate. Beat until thick. Pour into cooled pie shell. Refrigerate 15 minutes; add whipped cream to which 2 tablespoons sugar has been added. Chill until serving time.

Sweet Potato Pie

2 (16-ounce) cans sweet potatoes
1/3 cup light brown sugar
1/4 cup margarine
1 cup crushed pineapple
1-1/2 teaspoons cinnamon
Miniature marshmallows

Heat sweet potatoes in saucepan. Mash. Combine remaining ingredients; add to sweet potatoes. Pour into baking dish; cover with miniature marshmallows. Heat until marshmallows are light brown. Serve warm.

Apple Crumb Pie

6-7 tart apples
1-1/4 cups sugar
3/4 cup plus 2 tablespoons flour
1 tablespoon cinnamon
Dash of nutmeg
Dash of salt
1/2 cup butter

Slice apples; mix with 3/4 cup sugar, 2 tablespoons flour, cinnamon, nutmeg and salt. Put mixture in pie plate. Make crumbs by mixing 1/2 cup sugar, 3/4 cup flour together. Cut butter in flour and sugar. Sprinkle over top of apples. Bake at 400 degrees for 40 minutes or until done.

Peanut Butter Pie

4-ounces cream cheese
1 cup powdered sugar
1/2 cup plus 2 tablespoons peanut butter
9-ounce carton Cool Whip
Graham cracker pie shell
1 cup peanuts, chopped

Whip cream cheese and powdered sugar till fluffy. Beat in peanut butter. Fold in whipped topping. Pour into pie shell. Sprinkle with chopped nuts and additional Cool Whip if desired. You may double amounts for larger pie, except Cool Whip.

Esther's Coconut Pie

1 cup sugar
1/4 cup plain flour
3 large egg yolks
2 cups whole milk (no skim)
1/2 cup coconut
1/4 teaspoon coconut extract
1 baked pie crust

Mix sugar and flour together well; add 1/2 cup milk, mix. Add 3 well beaten egg yolks; add remainder of milk. Beat 1 minute. Microwave for 4 minutes; stir. Microwave 2 more minutes; stir. Cook 2 more minutes; add 1/2 cup coconut and coconut extract. Pour into baked pie crust. Top with meringue (recipe on page 93) and sprinkle 1/4 cup coconut on top. Brown in 350 oven till brown.

Esther Howard

95

Apple or Peach Strudel

Apples or peaches
Sugar
Cinnamon
Butter
1 cup sugar
1 teaspoon baking powder
1 cup flour
1/2 teaspoon salt (optional)
1 egg

In a buttered 9" square or 11x13" baking dish, put thick layer of fruit. Sprinkle with sugar and cinnamon (nutmeg if you like). Dot with butter. Mix together 1 cup sugar, baking powder, flour and salt. Add 1 egg; mix until crumbly. Spread over fruit. Bake at 350-375 degrees until brown, about 20-30 minutes. You an double the crumbs if you use a larger dish. This is good and easy!

Raisin Pie

3 eggs
1 cup sugar
2/3 cup nuts
1 cup raisins
1/2 cup margarine
1 teaspoon vinegar or lemon juice
1 teaspoon vanilla
1 unbaked pie shell

Cream sugar and margarine; add egg yolks, vinegar or lemon juice. Add nuts and raisins.

Beat egg whites; fold into mixture. Pour into pie shell. Bake in 325 degree oven until brown on top.

Frankie's Cafeteria Egg Custard

5 eggs (well beaten)
2 cups rich milk
1 cup sugar
1/2 cup butter
1 teaspoon vanilla
Nutmeg to taste
1 unbaked pie shell

Cream butter and sugar; add eggs. Beat until sugar dissolves. Add milk, vanilla and nutmeg. Bake at 450 degrees for 10 minutes, then 350 degrees until firm, about 45 minutes.

Apple Poke Pie

4 large tart apples
1 cup sugar
1/2 cup butter
9" unbaked pie shell
1 teaspoonn cinnamon
3/4 cup flour
1 large brown grocery bag

Peel and core apples. Arrange in bottom of pie shell. Mix 1/2 cup sugar and cinnamon. Sprinkle over apples. Sift rest of sugar with flour. Cut in butter until crumbly. Sprinkles over apples. Place in bag; bake 50-60 minutes at 375 degrees.

Pickle Barrel Strawberry Pie

4 tablespoons cornstarch

3 tablespoons strawberry jello

1 cup sugar

1 cup water

Mix ingredients and thicken in microwave. Add 4-5 drops red food coloring if desired. Cool; add 1 pint sliced strawberries. Pour into cool baked pie crust. Place in refrigerator to set up. Top with Cool Whip; serve

Janis Mack, owner
Pickles Gap Village
Conway, Arkansas

Apple Dumplings

Your favorite double crust pastry recipe

6 whole large apples, peeled and cored

1-1/2 cups sugar, divided

3/4 teaspoon cinnamon, divided

1/4 teaspoon nutmeg

6 tablespoons butter, divided

Roll out pastry 1/8" thick; cut into six 7" squares. Place an apple in the center of each square. Fill the apples with a mixture of 1/2 cup sugar, 1/2 teaspoon cinnamon, 1/4 teaspoon nutmeg and 2 tablespoons butter. Moisten edges of the pastry with cold water; fold them up around the apples, pressing the edges together to seal firmly. Prick the pastry in several places. Chill one hour. Combine remaining sugar, cinnamon, butter and 2 cups hot water; boil 5 minutes. Place apples in 9x12" baking dish. Bake in 450 degree preheated oven for 10 minutes. Reduce heat to 350 degrees; pour syrup over the apples and bake 35 minutes, basting occasionally. Makes 6 servings.   Becky Poe

Sour Cream Raisin Pie

1 cup light brown sugar, packed

2 tablespoons flour

1 teaspoon allspice

1 cup sour cream

3 egg yolks

3 tablespoons buttermilk

1 teaspoon vanilla

1 cup raisins, chopped

9" pie shell, unbaked

Combine sugar, spice and flour. Mix well; add sour cream, beaten egg yolks, buttermilk and vanilla; pour into unbaked pie shell. Bake 45-50 minutes at 350 degrees.

Esther Howard

When your work speaks for itself, don't interrupt."

97

Chocolate Chip Pie

1/4 cup plus 2 table-
spoons butter, softened
1 cup sugar
1 teaspoon vanilla
2 eggs
1/2 cup flour
6-ounce package chocolate chips
3/4 cup pecans, chopped
1/2 cup coconut
1 unbaked pie shell

Combine butter, sugar, vanilla; beat well. Add eggs and flour. Stir in chips, nuts and coconut. Pour in pie crust. Bake 30-40 minutes at 350 degrees.

Sin Pie

Layer 1: Crust:
1 stick margarine
1 cup flour
1/2 cup chopped nuts
Layer 2:
8-ounce package cream cheese
1/2 large Cool Whip
1 cup powdered sugar
Layer 3:
2 packages butterscotch instant pudding
3 cups milk
Mix until thick.
Layer 4:
Remaining Cool Whip

Layer 1: Mix and spread in large cake pan. Bake at 350 degrees until golden brown. **Layer 2:** Mix and spread on top of cooled crust. **Layer 3:** Mix pudding and milk, stir until thick. **Layer 4:** Spread remaining Cool Whip on pudding mixture, refrigerate. (You'll "sin" because you can't stop eating this pie.)

Esther Howard

No Bake Banana Pudding

1 large package instant
vanilla pudding and pie filling
3 or 4 bananas, sliced
Banana flavoring, optional
1 large carton Cool Whip,
reserve some for top
Vanilla wafer cookies

Make pudding as directed on package. Mix Cool Whip with pudding. Layer large casserole dish with vanilla wafer cookies and sliced bananas. Pour half of pudding mixture over that; add another layer of sliced bananas and top with remaining mixture. Crumble some vanilla wafers and a hand full of pecan pieces on top. Garnish with dots of Cool Whip and strawberries for a pretty dessert. You can also place vanilla wafers around the sides of the dish like a crust. I usually use 3-4 bananas for this recipe and sometimes add a little banana flavoring.

Janis Mack

Salads, Sauces & Dressings

Who knows, if you visit the Conway or Pickles Gap area around the first of May during "Toad Suck Daze Festival", you just might find a frog in your salad. Things get a little crazy about that time every year. Look for the "Legend of Toad Suck" in this book. Toad Suck T-shirts available from our mail order brochure, write or call 501-327-7708. (Address in back!)

It's feeding time! When one of our little critters is under the weather, Nurse Janis is there to lend a helping hand.

Friends and family enjoy the food and fellowship at Pickles Gap Village.

Frog Eye Salad

1 cup sugar

2 teaspoons flour

1/4 teaspoon salt

2 eggs, beaten

1-3/4 cups pineapple juice (from canned fruit)

3 teaspoons lemon juice

3 quarts salted water

1 teaspoon oil

1 package acini de pepe noodles

2 (11-ounce) cans mandarin oranges

2 (20-ounce) cans chunk pineapple

1 cup mini marshmallows

1 cup coconut

13-ounce carton Cool Whip

Cook first 5 ingredients until thick; add lemon juice. Cook acini de pepe until done; drain and rinse in cold water. Mix cooked mixture and acini; refrigerate overnight. Next day, drain fruit and add the rest of the ingredients to mixture. Serves a large group.

This would be a good salad to serve during **"TOAD SUCK DAZE FESTIVAL"** which is held the first weekend in May every year in Conway, Arkansas. It sponsors arts and crafts, fun games and a circus atmosphere to raise scholarship money for our three colleges.

We have a legend that tells the tale of old-timers sucking on their whiskey bottles until they swelled up like toads as they would frequent the old tavern that once was located along the Arkansas River just west of Conway on the Faulkner and Perry County lines. As a result, the community is called Toad Suck. The Corp of Engineers operates a beautiful park located near the lock and dam. It is the site of many family outings and picnics.

Toad Suck T-shirts and souvenirs are available at Pickles Gap Village. Write for mail order brochure, address in back of cook book!

99

Pickle Barrel Chicken Salad Low-Fat

6 boneless chicken breasts

Salt to taste and boil until done. Cool and chop.

Add:

1/2 cup white or red grapes, sliced

1/4 cup slivered almonds

1/2 cup diced apple with peel

You can add more of each of the above if so desired. Mix well; add enough low-fat salad dressing to blend flavors; add a dash or two of lemon pepper and a little fruit juice from any canned fruit. Great sandwich or good served on bed of lettuce.

Maxine Brinsfield & Janis Mack

Chicken salad is a favorite at the Pickle Barrel Restaurant at Pickles Gap Village, Conway, AR

Low-Fat Fruit Salad Deluxe

15-1/4 ounce can pineapple chunks, drained

16-ounce can dark sweet pitted cherries, drained

11-ounce can mandarin oranges, drained

1 cup green seedless grapes

1 cup fat-free sour cream

1/2 cup sugar

1/2 teaspoon vanilla extract

3-ounce package dry banana instant pudding mix

2 cups miniature marshmallows

In large bowl, combine all fruit. With electric mixer, blend sour cream, sugar and vanilla until sugar is dissolved. Pour over fruit and stir. Add dry instant pudding mix; blend. Fold in marshmallows; chill and serve. Makes 8 servings.

Low-Fat Buttermilk Coleslaw

6 cups raw cabbage, shredded

1/2 medium green pepper, chopped fine

1/2 cup carrot, shredded

1/8 teaspoon celery seed

Dressing:

1 cup fat-free mayonnaise

3/4 cup low-fat buttermilk

1/4 cup sugar

Salt to taste

In large bowl, mix cabbage, green pepper, carrot and celery seed. In a small bowl, gradually add buttermilk to mayonnaise. Mix in sugar gradually. Add salt. Pour dressing over cabbage. Mix well. Refrigerate. Makes 8-10 servings.

Low-Fat Pimento Chicken Salad

Salad:

2 cups cooked white chicken chunks

1 small onion, chopped

1 stalk celery, chopped

2 tablespoons pimento, chopped

1 apple, chopped

1/2 cup fat-free Monterey Jack cheese, grated

Salt to taste

Dressing:

1/2 cup fat-free Miracle Whip

1/3 cup fat-free cream cheese

In large bowl, combine salad ingredients. In small bowl, mix all dressing ingredients until thoroughly blended. Pour over salad; chill 1-2 hours before serving. Makes 6 servings.

Low-Fat Spaghetti Salad

10-ounces spaghetti, cooked and drained

4 slices turkey bacon, cooked and crumbled

1 cup chopped broccoli, lightly steamed

3/4 cup carrots, chopped, lightly steamed

Half of 10-ounce package frozen green peas

1 small purple onion, chopped

3 stalks celery, chopped

1 teaspoon garlic salt

1/2 teaspoon seasoned salt

16-ounce bottle Kraft Fat-Free Honey Dijon salad dressing

In large bowl, combine all ingredients except salad dressing. Mix and toss ingredients; add half bottle of dressing; toss. Chill. Just before serving, add remaining dressing and mix. Serves 8

Peach Pickle Salad

3-ounce package lemon jello

3-ounce package orange jello

1 cup hot water

3 cups juice from fruits

17-ounce can bing cherries

8-1/4 ounce can crushed pineapple

29-ounce can spiced peaches

1 cup pecans, broken

Dissolve both packages of jello in hot water. Stir in juice from the fruits. Cool. Add fruit and pecans. Allow to congeal in refrigerator. Serve with mayonnaise. Serves 10-12.

Orange Spinach Toss

4 cups spinach leaves, torn
3 oranges, peeled and sectioned
(may use mandarin oranges)
4 slices crisp, crumbled bacon
1/4 to 1/2 cup peanuts, chopped
1 envelope French dressing mix
(prepare as directed)

In salad bowl, combine spinach, oranges, bacon and peanuts. Mix and pour dressing over mixture. Serve immediately. Serves 4.

Cherry Salad

1 can cherry pie filling
1 can Eagle Brand milk
1 carton Cool Whip
1 can crushed pineapple, drained*
1 cup pecans

Mix together and chill before serving. For a variety, add 1/2 cup coconut to mixture before chilling.   *Janis Mack*
*This is a favorite at
the Pickle Barrel Restaurant,
Pickles Gap Village!*
*P.S. We save the pineapple juice for our chicken salad!

Banana and Strawberry Salad

2 packages strawberry flavored gelatin
2-1/2 cups boiling water
1 small package frozen strawberries
3 bananas, sliced
1/2 cup pecans, chopped
1/2 pint sour cream

Dissolve gelatin in boiling water. Add strawberries; stir until thawed. Add bananas and pecans. Pour half of mixture into an 8x8x2" pan; store in refrigerator until firm. Gel remaining half only to thick pouring consistency. Spread sour cream on first mixture; pour remaining half of mixture on top. Refrigerate till set.
Janis Mack

Lime Jello Salad

1 package lime jello
1/2 cup cold water
1 small can crushed pineapple
5 tablespoons sugar
Juice of 1 lemon
1/2 cup grated cheese
1/2 cup grated carrots
1/2 cup chopped pecans
1 package Dream Whip (as directed on package)

Dissolve jello in cold water. In a saucepan, mix sugar, pineapple, and lemon juice; bring to boil. Add jello; mix and chill until it thickens. Add cheese, carrots, nuts, and fold in whipped topping.
Nancy Mallett

Hot Potato Salad

6 cups cooked, diced potatoes
In a small saucepan, add:
1/2 cup sugar
2 tablespoons mayonnaise
1 teaspoon celery seed
1/4 cup vinegar
2 eggs
1 tablespoon mustard

Cook over low heat, stirring till thick. Pour over potatoes; mix until potatoes are covered with mixture. Serve warm.

Potato Salad

1 cup onions, chopped
1/2 cup mayonnaise
1 tablespoon sugar or Sweet & Low
1/4 teaspoon pepper
1 tablespoon margarine
1/3 cup vinegar
1-3/4 teaspoons salt
4 cups boiled or baked potatoes, cut up

Cook onions in margarine for 2-3 minutes. Stir in next 5 ingredients. Add potatoes and continue to cook, stirring about 2 minutes or until heated. Do not boil. Delicious!

Hot Chicken Salad

4 cups chicken, cooked & diced
2/3 cup chopped toasted almonds
1 teaspoon salt
2 pimentos, cut fine
2 cups celery, chopped
3/4 cup cream of chicken soup
1-1/2 cups potato chips, crushed
2 tablespoons lemon juice
3/4 cup mayonnaise
1/2 teaspoon Accent
1 cup cheese, grated
4 hard boiled eggs, diced
1 teaspoon onion, finely minced

Combine all ingredients except cheese, potato chips and almonds. Put in a 8x12" baking dish. Top with cheese, potato chips and almonds. Let stand overnight in the refrigerator. Bake at 400 degrees for 25 minutes. Serves 8 to 12.

Dorito Salad

1 pound ground beef
1 head lettuce, torn
3 tomatoes, diced
1 can red kidney beans
1 package taco seasoning
1 avocado, diced
4-ounces Cheddar cheese, diced
1 bottle Catalina Dressing

Brown meat in skillet; drain. Mix in taco seasoning; stir. Set aside. In large bowl combine remaining ingredients. Add meat mixture; mix well. Add one bag Dorito chips broken up. Serve

Sweet Spinach Salad

Fresh spinach

Sesame seed nuts

Fresh, sliced mushrooms

2-3 hard boiled eggs

6 slices cooked bacon, crumbled

Remove stems from spinach; wash leaves, pat dry. Tear into bite size pieces. Combine all above ingredients in bowl.

Dressing:

1 cup oil

1/4 cup wine vinegar

1 tablespoon Worcestershire

1 teaspoon salt

1/3 cup ketchup

1 tablespoon onion, minced

1/2 cup sugar

Put all above in blender; blend on low until mixed and onion is finely chopped. Serve over salad.   **Becky Poe**

Orange Cream Fruit Salad

20-ounce can pineapple tidbits, drained

16-ounce can peach slices, drained

11-ounce can mandarin oranges, drained

2 medium firm bananas, sliced

1 medium apple, chopped

3.4-ounce package instant vanilla pudding

1-1/2 cups milk

1/3 cup frozen orange juice concentrate

3/4 cup sour cream

Combine fruits in a large salad bowl. Set aside. In a small mixing bowl, beat pudding mix, milk and orange juice concentrate for 2 minutes. Add sour cream; mix well. Spoon over fruit; toss to coat. Cover and refrigerate for 2 hours. Serves 8-10.

Apple Ham Salad

2 tablespoons mayonnaise

1/4 teaspoon prepared mustard

1/2 teaspoon honey

1/2 teaspoon lemon juice

Dash ground cloves

1/2 cup julienned fully cooked ham

1 small apple, diced

1 celery rib, sliced

Lettuce leaves, optional

1/4 teaspoon sesame seeds, toasted

In a bowl, blend the first 5 ingredients. Stir in ham, apple and celery. Cover and refrigerate for 1 hour. Serve on a bed of lettuce. Sprinkle with sesame seeds. Yield: 1 serving.

Refrigerator Slaw

1 medium cabbage, shredded

1 onion, sliced thin

1 green pepper, sliced

1 carrot, sliced

1 cup sugar

Dressing:

1 cup white vinegar

1/2 cup salad oil

1 teaspoon celery seed

1 teaspoon dry mustard

1 teaspoon salt

Prepare vegetables in large bowl. Sprinkle sugar on top. Boil other ingredients 1 minute. Pour hot mixture over vegetables. Cover; let stand in refrigerator 4 hours or overnight. Will keep 2-3 weeks.   *Jean Sawrie*

Spicy Peach Salad

1 large can sliced peaches, drained

1/4 teaspoon cinnamon

2 tablespoons vinegar

Peach syrup

6-ounce size peach jello

1/4 cup sugar

1/8 teaspoon cloves

2 cups boiling water

Dissolve jello, sugar and spices in boiling water. Stir in peach syrup and vinegar. Add peaches; chill until firm.

Cranberry Salad

1 pound cranberries (grind in blender/food chopper)

1 cup sugar

3/4-pound miniature marshmallows

1 medium can crushed pineapple, drained

1 pint cream, whipped

1 cup nuts, chopped

Combine cranberries, pineapple and sugar. Let set 2 hours. Mix in whipped cream and marshmallows. Let set another 2 hours. Add nuts at serving time.

Cranberry Salad

2 cups cranberries

1 orange

1-1/2 cups sugar

1 cup nuts, chopped

1/2 cup celery, chopped

1 cup apples, chopped

Wash and drain cranberries. Add orange and grind together. Add sugar. Chill overnight. Next day drain in a strainer. Reserve the liquid. Dissolve any flavor red jello in 1 cup hot water. When cool, add reserved liquid plus nuts, celery and apples. Chill. This will keep for weeks.

Millionaire Salad

1 small package miniature marshmallows
1 cup nuts, chopped
Sugar to taste
8-ounces cream cheese
16-ounce can crushed pineapple, drained
1 small bottle maraschino cherries, chopped
2 cartons whipping cream

Put marshmallows, pineapple, nuts, cherries, cream cheese (cut into small squares) in bowl. Add whipped whipping cream. Keep refrigerated.

Rice Salad

3 cups cooked, cooled rice
1/2 cup sweet pickle or relish
1 cup mayonnaise
2-ounces pimento, chopped (optional)
1/2 cup green onions, chopped
Salt to taste
1 teaspoon prepared mustard
4 hard boiled eggs
Any chopped meat you may have on hand, optional

Mix the above together. Serve.

Hawaiian Rice

2 cups rice, cooked
1-1/2 cups marshmallows
1 cup crushed pineapple
Nuts, if desired

1 package strawberry jello
1 small bottle maraschino cherries
1/2 cup sugar
1/2 pint whipping cream, whipped

Mix all ingredients except cream. Refrigerate 4 hours before folding in whipped cream.

Carrot Salad

1 large package carrots
1 large bell pepper, chopped
1/2 cup oil
1/2 cup sugar
1 large onion, sliced
1 can tomato soup
1/2 cup vinegar

Slice carrots; boil in salted water 15 minutes or until slightly tender; drain. Heat oil, vinegar, sugar and tomato soup to a boil. Remove from heat; add carrots. Cool, add onion and pepper. Chill overnight.

Cranberry Salad

1 pound ground raw cranberries
1 can crushed pineapple, drained
3/4 to 1 cup sugar
1 pint whipping cream
1/2 pound miniature marshmallows

Mix first 3 ingredients; let stand 2 hours. Mix whipping cream and marshmallows. Combine ingredients; serve. Nuts may be added if desired.

Monta Langford

Green Vegetable Salad

1 head broccoli
1 head cauliflower
1 bell pepper
1 diced onion
1 large cucumber
1/2 stalk celery
1 can whole kernel corn, if desired
Italian Salad Dressing

Chop and combine first 6 ingredients; add corn. Sprinkle lightly with black pepper and garlic salt. Marinate overnight with Italian dressing.

Candied Pear Salad

3-ounce package cream cheese
1/4 cup Miracle Whip salad dressing
3/4 cup candied fruit, chopped
2 (1-pound) cans pear halves, drained
Lettuce

Combine softened cream cheese and salad dressing, mixing until well blended. Stir in candied fruit. For each salad, arrange 2 pear halves on lettuce. Top with salad dressing mixture; garnish with candied cherries. Serves 6-8.   *Pete Pleva*

Mexican Salad

1 pound hamburger, browned
1 pound cheese, grated
2 tomatoes, sliced
8-ounce bottle Catalina dressing
1 head lettuce, torn
2 (15-ounce) cans Ranch Style Beans
1/2 cup onion, chopped
6-1/2 ounce package Fritos, crushed

Drain beans and chill. Toss all ingredients except Fritos 30 minutes to one hour before serving. Add crushed Fritos just before serving. Serve with rolls and fruit salad.

German Slaw

Chop and mix 1 large cabbage, 1 bell pepper or carrot and 1 large onion. Sprinkle 1 cup sugar on top. Combine 1 cup vinegar, 2 tablespoons salt, 1 cup cooking oil and 1 tablespoon celery seed; heat to boil. Pour over cabbage mixture. Chill in covered bowl.

Sweet and Sour Sauce

1/2 cup dietetic jelly - apple or grape
2 tablespoons prepared mustard
Dissolve jelly in the top of a double boiler; stir in mustard. Mixture will re-congeal.

107

Low-Fat Quick Creamy Alfredo Sauce

1 cup evaporated skim milk

1/4 cup liquid Butter Buds

1/4 cup flour

4 teaspoons chicken broth

1/4 cup Parmesan cheese

1/4 teaspoon garlic, minced

1/4 teaspoon ground pepper

1/4 teaspoon lite salt (optional)

In small saucepan over low heat blend first 4 ingredients. Add garlic, salt and pepper. Continue to cook until sauce thickens. Stir in cheese; serve immediately. Serve with cooked fettuccine (10-12 ounces, cooked). Serves 6

Low-Fat Hollandaise Sauce

2 tablespoons liquid Butter Buds

1 cup boiling water

1/2 teaspoon lite salt (optional)

1 tablespoon flour

2 Egg Beaters, beaten

Juice of 1/2 lemon

Combine Butter Buds and flour in saucepan. Add boiling water; stir constantly. Cook over low heat. Beat Egg Beaters, salt and lemon juice together. Add some of the first mixture to this before slowly adding to the Butter Buds, flour and water. Cook until the spoon is well coated. This is delicious, easy to make, and will keep well. It is just as good warmed over as it is fresh off the stove. Makes 1-1/2 cups.

Low Calorie Ketchup

1/2 teaspoon grated onion

1/8 teaspoon ketchup spices

3 tablespoons water

2 tablespoons vinegar

6 quarter-grain saccharin tablets or other sweetener to equal same

1/8 teaspoon ground cloves

3/4 teaspoon salt

6-ounce can tomato paste, not concentrated

Place water, vinegar, onion and spices in pan. Bring to a boil; simmer 5 minutes. Remove from stove; add tomato paste, salt and saccharin tablets. Mix well; store in refrigerator. One tablespoon equals 17 calories.

Barbecue Sauce

1 cup water
4 tablespoons granulated sugar
1 teaspoon salt
1 medium onion, chopped
4 tablespoons Worcestershire
1/2 cup vinegar
4 teaspoons prepared mustard
1 teaspoon black pepper
1 cup ketchup

Mix all ingredients in large skillet or pan; simmer 30 minutes. Serve over cooked, chopped pork or beef for a great sandwich.

Favorite Dressing

2 cups Miracle Whip Salad Dressing
1/4 cup vinegar
1 teaspoon chili powder
1 cup ketchup
1/2 cup sugar
1 teaspoon garlic powder

Mix by hand or mixer; chill. Makes 2/3-quart. Keep well.

Cucumber Sauce

1 cup mayonnaise
1/2 cup cucumber, finely diced
2 tablespoons bell pepper, diced
1/2 teaspoon salt
1 teaspoon tarragon vinegar
Dash cayenne pepper

Combine all ingredients. Chill and serve over lettuce salad.

Russian Dressing

1 cup salad oil
1 cup ketchup
1/3 cup sugar
3 tablespoons vinegar
1 tablespoon onion, diced
3 tablespoons bell pepper, diced
1 teaspoon celery seed
1 teaspoon salt
1/4 teaspoon pepper

Put all ingredients in a jar and shake well. Chill. Makes 2-1/2 cups.

Sour Cream Dressing

8-ounces sour cream
3/4 cup mayonnaise
1-3/4 teaspoons garlic salt
1-1/2 teaspoons coarsely cracked black pepper
3 tablespoons Parmesan cheese, grated
3 tablespoons milk

Mix all ingredients. Use more milk as needed to thin dressing to desired consistency. Makes 2 cups. Recipe may be multiplied by 10 to yield 1-3/4 gallons.

Thousand Island Dressing

1 cup mayonnaise
1 teaspoon paprika
1/4 cup ketchup or chili sauce
2 tablespoons vinegar
1/2 cup celery, chopped
1/2 cup stuffed olives, sliced
1 small onion, chopped
2 tablespoons minced parsley
3 hard-boiled eggs, diced

Combine all ingredients. Chill. Makes 2-1/2 cups.

Bread Pudding Sauce

4 heaping tablespoons sour cream
1/2 cup sugar
1/2 stick butter or margarine

Cream all ingredients and heat. When hot add:
2 teaspoons lemon juice
Raisins, to taste

For different flavor, leave out lemon juice and raisins; add 1/4 cup frozen orange juice, thawed. This is also good over hot dinner rolls-it will turn them into a sweet bread.

Maxine Brinsfield

Green Bean Sauce

2 cups mayonnaise
1 small onion, chopped
1 teaspoon prepared mustard
6 tablespoons olive oil
1 teaspoon Worcestershire
1/8 teaspoon Tabasco sauce
4 hard cooked eggs

Place all in blender bowl; blend 1-2 seconds, just until onion is grated. Pour over cooked green beans.

Becky Poe

Coffee Walnut Sauce

1/2 cup triple-strength coffee
1-1/2 teaspoons cornstarch
1/2 cup honey
1 tablespoon brandy
1 teaspoon grated orange rind
1/2 cup walnuts, chopped

Combine coffee and cornstarch; add honey, brandy and orange rind. Cook over medium heat, stir constantly till sauce boils. Reduce heat; simmer 1 minute. Add walnuts. Cool; refrigerate - yield: 1 cup sauce.

Hot Mocha Sauce

3 tablespoons unsalted butter
3-ounces unsweetened chocolate
1/2 cup strong coffee
1/4 cup light corn syrup
1 cup sugar
Pinch of salt
1 teaspoon vanilla

In a saucepan, melt butter and chocolate. Add coffee, corn syrup, sugar and salt. Bring to a boil. Boil gently, without stirring, till thick and smooth. Add vanilla. Serve hot. Makes 1 cup.

This is our "Fun Section". You'll find a few recipes, photos taken at Pickles Gap Village and other surprises. Hope you will take time to visit Pickles Gap Village while traveling Arkansas. It's a fun place for the entire family.

Ralph, monkey and friends riding the stage coach in the
Faulkner County parade in Conway, Arkansas.

We often have visitors at Pickles Gap Village who have to
be kept on a leash!

Sweetened Condensed Milk

1 cup instant nonfat dry milk

2/3 cup sugar

1/2 cup boiling water

3 tablespoons melted margarine

Combine all ingredients in blender. Process until smooth. Makes 1-1/4 cups or 1 can.

Scalloped Pineapple

20-ounce can chunk pineapple in its own juice

14-ounce can chunk pineapple in its own juice

2 sticks margarine, melted

4 eggs, well beaten

2-2/3 cups sugar

1/4 cup brown sugar

4 hamburger buns

Crumble buns; mix with melted margarine. Mix sugar with beaten eggs. Add other ingredients. Bake at 400 degrees until it starts bubbling. Reduce heat to 350 degrees; cook about 25-30 minutes. Good to serve with ham.

Esther Howard

"A sense of humor is what makes you laugh at something which would make you mad if it happened to you."

Honey Butter

1/2 cup butter, softened

1/2 cup honey

Beat butter at high speed of electric mixer until creamy. Gradually add honey and beat until blended. Pour into a covered container and refrigerate. Makes 1 cup.

Seasoned Salt

1 cup salt

2 tablespoons celery salt

2 tablespoons garlic salt

2 tablespoons paprika

2 teaspoons dry mustard

2 teaspoons onion powder

2 teaspoons pepper

Place all ingredients in blender. Blend 20 seconds on high. Store in tightly covered container.

Chocolate Gravy

3 tablespoons flour

3/4 cup sugar

1 teaspoon vanilla

2 tablespoons cocoa

2 cups milk

Combine flour, cocoa and sugar in saucepan. Stir in milk; bring to boil. Boil until slightly thickened. Remove from heat and add vanilla. Serve with hot buttered biscuits. A Sunday morning favorite at our house.

Charlotte Roberts

Healthy Granola

2 tablespoons light corn oil spread

1 cup uncooked oats

1/4 cup sliced almonds

3 tablespoons Grapenut flakes

2 tablespoons brown sugar, packed

1 tablespoon unsalted sunflower seeds

1/2 cup raisins

Heat oven to 375 degrees. Place corn oil spread in 9-inch square baking pan. Heat in oven until melted (1 to 2 minutes). Meanwhile, stir next 5 ingredients in bowl until blended. Pour into pan with melted corn oil spread and toss. Bake 15 to 20 minutes until golden; stirring occasionally. Stir in raisins and cool completely. Store in airtight container for up to one month. Makes 2 cups.

Janis Mack

Company Potatoes

5 pounds potatoes, cooked and prepared like mashed potatoes

8-ounces cream cheese

8-ounces sour cream

1 tablespoon garlic juice

Mix all ingredients with electric mixer. Pour into baking dish; cover with foil. Bake at 350 degrees for approximately 30 minutes. Remove foil and add grated cheese. Return to oven until melted.

April Mack

(April is a sweet daughter-in-law, the mother of my beautiful granddaughters.'')

Janis Mack

Chinese Chicken and Vegetables

4 chicken breasts, skinned

16-ounces frozen Oriental vegetables

1 can cream of mushroom soup

1 small can pimentos

1/3 cup soy sauce

Salt and garlic salt to taste

In 2-quart casserole, put chicken breasts, vegetables, soup, pimentos, soy sauce and salts. Mix well. Bake at 350 degrees for 1 hour.

Ralph Mack

"Opportunity, they say, is like a horse. It gallops up to you from nowhere and pauses. Now it's time to get on. If you don't, he'll soon be gone and the clatter of his hoofs will be heard dying away in the distance."

Author Unknown

112

Souped-Up
Chicken and Dressing
with Giblet Gravy

1 stewing hen

1 quart water

1 teaspoon salt

4 eggs

6 cups cornbread crumbs

3 cups plain bread crumbs

3/4 cup onion, chopped

1/2 cup celery, chopped

2 tablespoons sage

5 cups seasoned chicken broth

10-1/2 ounce can cream of
chicken soup

1 raw egg

Cover hen with water; season with a teaspoon salt and any other desired seasoning. Simmer till tender (1-1/2 to 2 hours). Boil 4 eggs (2 for giblet gravy). Mix together bread crumbs, onion, celery and sage. Set aside. When chicken is done, remove the bones and separate meat from broth. Add enough water to broth to make five cups. Add the cream of chicken soup to the broth and bring to a boil. Pour 1/2 of the broth over bread mixture, stirring rapidly. Add raw egg, stirring it into the mixture; add remainder of broth. Add chicken chunks (about 3 cups) and 2 chopped boiled eggs. Mix well. (For creamier chicken and dressing, add soup last.) Place mixture in a 3 to 4-quart roasting pan and bake uncovered at 350 degrees for 30 to 40 minutes, until golden brown. Serve with Easy Giblet Gravy. Serves 12.

Easy Giblet Gravy:

10-1/2 ounce can cream of
chicken soup

3/4 cup water

3-ounce can chopped
mushrooms, drained

2 chopped boiled eggs

Dash of Kitchen Bouquet

Heat all ingredients in saucepan and serve hot, over dressing.

This was a winning recipe in the 1971 Arkansas Poultry Cooking Festival. Janis Mack was the 1971 Ozark District Queen. She took this recipe to the state cook off.

Ralph's English Beef Roast

1 large English roast
Salt
Pepper
Garlic salt
Worcestershire sauce
Chopped onion
Sliced mushrooms, fresh or canned
2 cups brewed coffee

Place roast in large roasting pan. Rub with salt, pepper and garlic salt. Dash with worcestershire sauce. Cover meat with chopped onion and sliced mushrooms. Pour two cups brewed coffee around roast. Cover and bake at 350 degrees until tender. (Coffee helps to make meat tender.) Thicken juice and make brown gravy to serve over roast.

Ralph Mack
(This is a favorite at the Pickle Barrel Restaurant, Pickles Gap Village.)

Potato Cheese Casserole

6 large potatoes
1/2 cup light margarine
2 cups light sour cream
1 teaspoon onion powder
2 cups light grated medium or sharp cheddar cheese

2 teaspoons salt
Pepper

Boil potatoes with jackets on. Let cool. Peel and grate. Mix melted margarine, sour cream and onion powder. Add to potatoes. Add salt, pepper and 1 cup cheese; mix well. Sprinkle remainder of cheese on top. Let set in refrigerator until flavors have blended - overnight or at least 6 hours. When ready to serve, bake 45 minutes at 350 degrees

Sharon Dillard

Bonnie's Rice

1 cup onion soup
1 cup (4-ounces) mushrooms
1 tablespoon soy sauce
1 tablespoon worcestershire
1 cup raw rice

Melt a stick of butter in casserole dish and add onion soup, mushrooms, soy sauce, worcestershire and rice. Stir and bake for 1 hour at 350 degrees.

Bonnie Patterson

114

Claudia's Stove Top Baked Beans

1 large can pork and beans
4 slices bacon
Brown sugar
Ketchup

Brown bacon in skillet; pour in pork and beans. Season with brown sugar and ketchup to taste. Start out wih a little of each and add to beans to suit your taste. Let simmer for a few minutes for flavors to mix. (If your family will eat onions, add a few chopped onion pieces and a little bell pepper for more flavor.) Pour into a baking dish and serve.

Claudia Hancock

Rice, Cheese and Broccoli Casserole

1 stick margarine
1 small onion, chopped
1 can cream of mushroom or chicken soup
1 cup water
1 medium box Velveeta cheese (shredded or cut up)
1 large bag frozen chopped broccoli
1-1/2 cups Minute Rice or regular rice, cooked
Dash of garlic powder

Sauté onions in melted margarine over medium heat. Add soup and water; stir until creamy. Add cheese and stir until smooth. Add broccoli and cook over low heat for approximately 10 minutes, stirring often. Add rice and garlic powder; mix and continue cooking over low heat for 3 minutes. Pour into casserole dish and serve. Garnish with shredded cheddar cheese. (NOTE: Mushrooms can be added when onions are saute ing for extra flavor. I use medium can of mushroom stems and pieces.)

Janis Mack

(A great hit when I serve it at the Pickle Barrel Restaurant at Pickles Gap Village.)

115

Maxine's Potato Soup

4 large potatoes
2 carrots
1 onion, small (diced)
4 chicken bouillon cubes
2 sticks margarine
4 tablespoons regular flour
1 pint Half & Half
Milk
6 to 8 slices American cheese
Dash of garlic salt
A few dashes of dried parsley
Salt and pepper to taste

Chop potatoes and carrots. Cover potatoes, carrots, and onion with water (3" to 4" above vegetables). Season with salt and pepper to taste and 4 cubes chicken bouillon (dissolved). While this is cooking, make a rue: 2 sticks melted margarine and 4 tablespoons regular flour. After vegetables are tender, add the rue to thicken. Add 1 pint Half and Half plus enough milk to thin down the soup to desired thickness. Add: 6 to 8 slices American cheese, dash of garlic salt and a few dashes dried parsley. When all ingredients have blended, taste to see if more salt and pepper is needed. Soup may thicken too much, just add more milk or water to thin. *Maxine Brinsfield*
This is a favorite soup served at the Pickle Barrel Restaurant at Pickles Gap Village. Great with our Cotten Picken Corn Bread Muffins. Look in the bread section for that recipe!

Quick Chicken and Dumplings

1 large chicken or small hen
Salt and pepper to taste
1 small package flour tortilllas
1 can cream of chicken soup

Salt and pepper chicken; let set for a few minutes. (Can cook chicken whole or cut-up.) Place chicken in large pot covered with water. Cook until done. Cool and de-bone chicken. Save broth. Heat broth to a boil; slowly drop tortillas that have been cut 1/4 to 1/2 inch long pieces to resemble noodles. Place them a few at a time (not all at once) into broth. (You may not use entire package of tortillas depending on how much broth you have.) They will cook very quickly. When done add cream of chicken soup (optional). Continue cooking until soup has blended with dumplings. Add chicken, stirring gently. For a great flavor, add a little poultry seasoning and lemon pepper seasoning to taste.

Esther Howard & Janis Mack
This is a favorite served often at the Pickle Barrel Restaurant!

116

HELPFUL HINTS for Microwaving

A stick of BUTTER (or MARGARINE) will *soften* in one minute when microwaved at 20% power.

Microwave *hardened* BROWN SUGAR in an open box with 1 cup of hot water on high for 1.5 to 2 minutes for a half pound ... 2 to 3 minutes for one pound.

To *scald* MILK, cook 1 cup milk for 2 to 2.5 minutes. Stir once for each minute.

To *refresh* stale POTATO CHIPS, CEREALS, CRACKERS, SNACKS ... put a plateful in microwave for 30 to 45 seconds. Let stand for 1 to 2 minutes.

To make DRY BREAD CRUMBS ... cut 5 to 6 slices of bread into half inch cubes. Microwave 6 to 7 minutes in 3-quart casserole (or until dry). Stir after a few minutes. Use blender to crush.

To *thaw* HAMBURGER, GROUND ROUND without parts starting to cook before it's defrosted... defrost about 3 minutes, remove outside portions, continue defrosting at short intervals ... removing portions until all is defrosted.

To *drain fat* from HAMBURGER while it is cooking in microwave ... cook in plastic colander placed inside casserole dish ... one pound cooks in 5 minutes on high.

MEATLOAF ... shaping into a ring will stop the center from undercooking.

CHOPPED VEGETABLES and CUBED MEAT should be *cut uniformily* for more even cooking.

To help *eliminate* meat-spoiling kinds of *bacteria*, microwave on high FRESH MEAT CUTS for 15 to 20 seconds.

To prepare CHICKEN *in a dish*, put the bony pieces in the center, meaty pieces around the edges.

To *soften* JELLO that set up too hard ... heat on low power for a few seconds.

To *soften* CREAM CHEESE ... one 8-oz. package for 2 to 2.5 minutes at 30% power ... one 3-oz. package for 1.5 to 2 minutes at 30% power.

To *soften* HARD ICECREAM ... one pint at 30% power for 15 to 30 seconds, one quart for 30 to 45 seconds, and one-half gallon for 45 to 60 seconds.

To *dissolve* GELATIN in microwave (requires less stirring) ... Measure liquid in measuring cup, add jello and heat.

To *thaw* WHIPPED TOPPING ... Using the defrost setting, one 4.5 ounce carton will thaw in 1 minute ... DO NOT OVERTHAW ... center should be slightly firm, but will blend when stirred!

To *thaw* FROZEN ORANGE JUICE right in its container ... remove the top metal lid ... place open container in microwave ... 6 ounce, heat 30 seconds on high ... 12 ounce, heat 45 seconds on high.

CAKES ... to make sure the bottom gets done, put cake dish on top of another dish or on a roasting rack. Also works for potatoes and other foods. Note: When baking cakes, if you use a round dish instead of a square one you will eliminate overcooking the corners.

To ensure *uniform baking* throughout when baking BROWNIES, LARGE CAKES, MOIST BARS ... place a juice glass in the center of the baking dish. Also keeps middle from being soggy.

Fill pans *only half full* when baking CAKES and QUICK BREADS since they rise higher in a microwave.

Sprinkle a layer of finely chopped medium *walnuts* onto the bottom and sides of pan evenly — pour in batter and microwave per directions ... enhances quality (and looks) of QUICK BREADS and CAKES prepared in microwave.

Left-over CUSTARD can be heated and used as *frosting* for a cake.

To *melt* MARSHMELLOW CREME ... 3.5 oz. will melt in 35 to 40 seconds ... stir.

To melt ALMOND BARK for candies (or dipping pretzels) ... 1 lb. for about 2 minutes, stirring a couple of times.

117

MEASUREMENTS
Equivalents in U.S. and Metric

U.S.	Equivalents	Metric* Volume-milliliters
Dash	less than 1/8 teaspoon	
1 teaspoon	60 drops	5 ml.
1 tablespoon	3 teaspoons	15 ml.
2 tablespoons	1 fluid ounce	30 ml.
4 tablespoons	1/4 cup	60 ml.
5 1/3 tablespoons	1/3 cup	80 ml.
6 tablespoons	3/8 cup	90 ml.
8 tablespoons	1/2 cup	120 ml.
10 2/3 tablespoons	2/3 cup	160 ml.
12 tablespoons	3/4 cup	180 ml.
16 tablespoons	1 cup or 8 ounces	240 ml.
1 cup	1/2 pint or 8 fluid ounces	240 ml.
2 cups	1 pint	480 ml.
1 pint	16 ounces	480 ml. or .473 liter
1 quart	2 pints	960 ml. or .95 liter
2.1 pints	1.05 quarts or .26 gallons	1 liter
2 quarts	1/2 gallon	
4 quarts	1 gallon	3.8 liters
		Weight-grams
1 ounce	16 drams	28 grams
1 pound	16 ounces	454 grams
1 pound	2 cups liquid	
1 kilo	2.20 pounds	

* Figures are rounded off. In cooking, the important thing to remember
  is to use relative amounts when measuring.

Avoid using raw eggs in homemade ice cream

This article was published in the
Log Cabin Democrat — *Conway, Ark., Tuesday, May 14, 1996*

By LAURA CONNERLY
Faulkner County Extension Service

Making ice cream is a favorite summertime activity for many people. If your favorite ice cream recipe uses uncooked eggs, it needs to be replaced or revised. Raw eggs may contain salmonella bacteria that can cause food borne illness.

Salmonella food poisoning (salmonellosis) usually results from eating contaminated food that has been improperly handled or not cooked thoroughly. Salmonella enteritidis is an unusual strain of salmonella that has been found in the ovaries of infected laying hens. The hens transmit the organism to the egg yolk before the shell forms; therefore, we can no longer assume that a clean, uncracked egg is safe to eat.

Freezing does not destroy salmonella bacteria that is present in the raw egg. Thorough cooking is necessary to destroy salmonella bacteria. This means that foods that contain raw or lightly cooked eggs are risky and should be avoided.

Homemade ice cream recipes that call for cooking the egg mixture are safe to use. These are sometimes referred to as cooked custard ice cream. Another option is to use pasteurized eggs in recipes that call for raw eggs. Commercial pasteurization destroys salmonella bacteria, but does not cook the eggs or affect their color, flavor, nutritional value or functional properties. Whole liquid pasteurized eggs are available at some supermarkets. They are packaged in containers that resemble a small milk carton and are in the refrigerator case.

Eggs are used in ice cream to add rich flavor and color, to inhibit ice crystallization and to help stabilize or emulsify the fat and liquid so that the product is smooth and creamy. Commercial manufacturers use pasteurized eggs, stabilizers and other substitute ingredients to produce a safe and acceptable product.

Although the risk of getting salmonellosis is relatively small, the infection can be life threatening for certain people, especially the very young, the elderly, pregnant women and people with weakened immune systems.

MISSING INGREDIENT SUBSTITUTIONS

1 sq. **chocolate** (1 ounce) = 3 or 4 tablespoons cocoa plus 1/2 tablespoon fat

3/4 cup **cracker crumbs** = 1 cup bread crumbs

1 cup sifted **all-purpose flour** = 1 cup plus 2 tablespoons sifted cake flour

1 cup sifted **cake flour** = 1 cup minus 2 tablespoons sifted all-purpose flour

1 cup **sour milk** = 1 cup sweet milk into which 1 tablespoon lemon juice or vinegar has been stirred; or 1 cup buttermilk — let stand for 5 minutes

1 cup **sweet milk** = 1 cup sour milk or buttermilk plus 1/2 teasp. baking soda

1 cup **cream, sour, heavy** = 1/3 cup butter and 2/3 cup milk in any sour milk recipe.

1 cup **whole milk** = 1/2 cup evaporated milk and 1/2 cup water or 1 cup reconstituted nonfat dry milk and 1 tablespoon butter

3 cups **dry corn flakes** = 1 cup crushed corn flakes

1/8 teaspoon **garlic powder** = 1 small pressed clove of garlic

1 teaspoon **baking powder** = 1/4 teaspoon baking soda plus 1/2 teaspoon cream of tartar

1 teaspoon **dried herbs** = 1 tablespoon fresh herbs

1 tablespoon **cornstarch** (for thickening) = 2 tablespoons flour

1 tablespoon **instant minced onion, rehydrated** = 1 small fresh onion

1 tablespoon **prepared mustard** = 1 teaspoon dry mustard

1 package **active dry yeast** = 1 cake compressed yeast

1 pound **whole dates** = 1 1/2 cups pitted and cut dates

3 medium **bananas** = 1 cup mashed bananas

10 miniature **marshmallows** = 1 large marshmallow

OVEN CHART

Very slow oven ...... 250° to 300° F	Slow oven ...... 300° to 325° F
Moderate oven ...... 325° to 375° F	Medium hot ...... 375° to 400° F
Hot oven ...... 400° to 450° F	Very hot oven ...... 450° to 500° F

Legends & Such

The Legend of Pickles Gap

This quaint little ozark village gets its unique name from the legend of a German immigrant crossing the creek and overturning his wagon load of pickles.

Long ago, steamboats traveled the Arkansas River when the water was the right depth. When it wasn't, the captains and their crews tied up to wait where Toad Suck Ferry Lock and Dam now spans the river. While they waited, they refreshed themselves at a tavern there, to the dismay of the folks living nearby, who said: "They suck on the bottle 'til they swell up like toads." Hence, Toad Suck. The tavern is long gone, but the legend lives on.

Toad Suck Daze Festival is celebrated in downtown Conway, Arkansas every year around the first weekend in May. It brings thousands of people into the area and money is raised for scholarships for our three colleges.

Conway is really jumping. . . Mayor David Kinley seems to be leading in the toad race (Toad Suck Daze-1996).

'Daze' founder recalls origin of festival name

(Editor's Note: Several individuals who have been involved in Toad Suck Daze in its 15-year existence were asked to write a short remembrance of the festival.)

By JOHN L. WARD
Special to the Log Cabin

The two guys responsible for Toad Suck Daze . . . Bill and John Ward of Ward Advertising.

I was determined to come up with a unique and memorable name for the celebration back there in the winter of 1981. Spring was sure to come and there would be the usual euphoria from the warm weather, the green grass, the singing of the birds and all that other stuff that goes with the season. How to capture that in the name for a springtime celebration? I had no idea.

But I zeroed in on the fact that with Toad Suck Ferry Lock and Dam just down the road, the name would need Toad Suck in it. But what else? I tried out perhaps a hundred names — Toad Suck Tangle, Toad Suck Tango, Toad Suck Trance, Toad Suck Travail, Toad Suck Trash (oops). I seemed to be hung up on having a "T" word at the end for some reason. I agonized for probably two weeks and drove everyone just about bonkers as I tried out this name or that on anyone who'd listen.

Finally, it hit me. "Toad Suck Days." I rolled it around all afternoon on my tongue and took it to bed with me. Next morning, some of the zing was gone. It didn't have in it the joy of spring, fellowship, fun and all that stuff.

"Daze" not "Days", stupid! That was it, the dizzy, euphoric, non-sensical state of mind that drives a young man's fancy and maybe everybody else's. Toad Suck Daze. It just somehow worked. I still like it.

123

Legend of Skunk Hollow. . . .
. . . .one of many

Years ago a family, looking for a peaceful place to settle down and raise their family, found a hollow just east of Conway, Arkansas. There they built a home, barn, and a chicken house. They had bad luck trying to raise chickens. Something kept breaking into the chicken house and catching their chickens.

Grandpa came to visit and brought along his steel bear traps. So, he decided to bait up the traps and catch the chicken thief. The next morning the traps were full of skunks!

The stink was so bad that neighbors from far and near came to check it out. You guessed it! Skunk Hollow was therefore named.

The skunks have long gone, but you might still find a two legged polecat (another name for skunk) or two still around in those parts.

Ralph and Janis Mack, husband and wife team for 38 years are the owners of Pickles Gap Village near Conway, Arkansas. They invite you to stop by and enjoy some fun shopping in the various antique, craft and gift shops. They serve great bar-b-que, and the homemade fudge is a must!

View of Pickles Gap Village from the duck pond.

"Our goats need your love." Kaleb and Alison are checking out a baby goat at Kiddie Land.

"Feeding our ducks will quack you up!"

Pickles Gap's Kiddie Land is a fun place for kids of all ages.

Grandpa Exel and one of our friendly critters at Kiddie Land - Pickles Gap Village.

Children having fun at Kiddie Land - Pickles Gap Village.

Everyone is fascinated with Bill and Hillary as they welcome visitors at Pickles Gap Village. They have a little help from Ralph who operates a microphone from inside the shop. What a fun place!!

Santa paying a visit to Mack's General Store.

129

Bonnie Patterson, manager Mack's General Store, showing one of our beautiful afghans.

Is Santa shopping for fudge or a hug from one of our pretty clerks at the Fudge Shop?

Rita, one of our talented artists, with a lovely Arkansas quilt from the Quilt Loft.

David Mack in his "Bull Pen", featuring sports cards and memorabilia. Kids of all ages love this shop at Pickles Gap Village!

Store manager, Mary Mack showing our World Traveler T-Shirt to a customer at Granny's Log Cabin - Pickles Gap Village.

Mary Mack loves selling Glenda Turley art and accessories at Granny's Log Cabin - Pickles Gap Village.

June welcomes you to browse the Treasure Hunt and Antiques at Pickles Gap Village. "Not the same ole' same ole'."

If it's antiques, collectibles you are looking for, check out The Village Store at Pickles Gap Village.

Mr. & Mrs. Paul Overstreet from Nashville, TN had lunch with friends at Pickles Gap Village.

TV sports announcer Paul Eells and his lovely wife, Vickie, enjoying some of Ralph's famous Bar-B-Q at Pickles Gap Village.

Look who stopped by for lunch at Pickles Gap . . . . Ramona and Grandpa Jones!

You can never tell who will show up at Pickles Gap Village looking for a rare antique. Yes! . . . she was here. (Tammy Faye and Janis Mack)

Pickles Gap Craft and Gift shops are full of neat things for shoppers to explore.

Janis Mack accepting the 1995 Travel Council Silver Cup Award from Lou Vitale. Janis is past president of the Arkansas Travel Council, 1994-95.

138

139

ORDER FORM

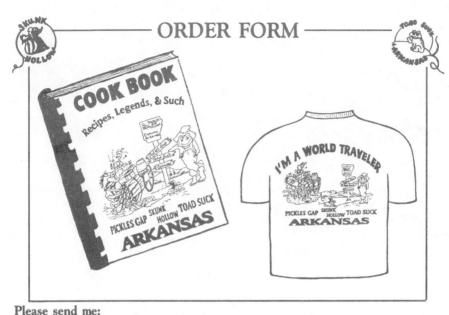

Please send me:

_____ copies of **Pickles Gap Cook Book** $ 9.95 ea. $_____

Plus postage and handling . . . . $ 2.50 ea. $_____

_____ **World Traveler T-Shirts** . . . . Adult $12.95 ea. $_____

_____ **World Traveler T-Shirts** . . . . Childrens $ 9.95 ea. $_____

Plus postage and handling . . . . $ 2.50 ea. $_____

Please circle: (Sorry, no choice in color)

adult size: **Small   Medium   Large**   Sub Total $_____

X-Large   XX-Large   5% tax $_____

child size: **Small   Medium   Large**   Total $_____
(2-4)   (6-8)   (10-12)
(Postage will be more outside the USA. Write or call: 501-329-9049)

Name_____

Address_____

City _____ State _____ Zip _____

Method of Payment: Check ☐   Money Order ☐   Visa ☐   MasterCard ☐

☐☐☐☐ ☐☐☐☐ ☐☐☐☐

Expiration Date _____ Signature _____

Make checks payable to:

PICKLES GAP VILLAGE

**5-A GAPVIEW ROAD
CONWAY, ARKANSAS 72032**

501-329-9049 or 501-327-7708